READER'S DIGEST
PRACTICAL HOME DECORATING

Curtains & Shades

READER'S DIGEST

PRACTICAL HOME DECORATING

Curtains & Shades

A Step-by-Step Guide to
Creative Window Treatments

Melanie Paine

Photographs by
Michael Crockett

READER'S DIGEST ASSOCIATION, INC.
Pleasantville, New York/Montreal

A READER'S DIGEST BOOK

Conceived, edited, and designed by
COLLINS & BROWN LIMITED

Library of Congress Cataloging in Publication Data

Paine, Melanie
    Curtains & shades : a step-by-step guide to creative window
treatments / Melanie Paine.
        p.   cm. — (Practical home decorating)
    Includes index.
    ISBN 0-89577-979-X
    1. Drapery.   2. Window shades.   3. Drapery in interior decoration.
I. Title.   II. Series.
TT390.P35 1997
646.2'1—dc21   97-22202

Editorial Director: Colin Ziegler
Editor: Jinny Johnson
Art Director: Roger Bristow
Designer: Sarah Davies
Style photography by Michael Crockett
Styling by Melanie Paine
Sets built by Steve Gott
Step-by-step photography by Sampson Lloyd and Geoff Dann
Illustrations by Ian Sidaway

Printed in Italy

CONTENTS

The Basic Techniques

The Projects

INTRODUCTION

IMAGINATIVE WINDOW FURNISHINGS can transform your home. The right style of curtain or shade is the quickest, simplest way of softening a stark interior, concealing an unpleasant view, or bringing new brightness and color to a room. Depending on your choice of fabric, curtains or shades can make a room look warm and cozy or create a cool, refreshing ambience. A curtain may be as simple as a sheer fabric threaded on a pole slot-head style (see pp. 60–63) or as ornate as a luxurious velvet with a contrasting gathered drape (see pp. 80–85). A plain Roman shade (see pp. 96–99) lends a classic subtlety while a more complex pleated shade (see pp. 118–23) becomes a focal point.

When you start making your own curtains and shades you will find that there is a vast and ever-changing array of fabrics available to inspire you. I find that keeping a collection of swatches is an ideal way of learning about fabrics. Look at as many varieties of color, pattern, texture, and weight as possible to help you appreciate what fabrics can and cannot do. Some, such as wool damask, drape particularly well and suggest gracious floor-length curtains, falling in soft folds. Crisp cottons hold their shape and are ideal for stylish shades. Don't be afraid to combine different types of fabric in one arrangement – in the right situation, opposites, such as velvet and silk taffeta, look wonderful. There are few hard and fast rules other than to keep a balance.

A window is not simply an arrangement of glass and timber. It frames your view of the outside world. It lets in light and contributes a great deal to the character of a room. Proportion plays an important part in styling windows, and it is best to be guided by what is there rather than try to distort it. Before you begin to make curtains or shades, assess the shape of your window (see pp. 8–9) and decide on the best approach. Then turn to the pages on choosing a style (see pp. 12–33) and browse through the array of types of support, headings, and fabrics to help you select what is right for your home. Decide if you want to have a chunky pole with decorative finials or a more discreet concealed support; look at the wide range of headings to chose from, and consider using embellishments, such as fringes and tiebacks.

The basic skills of making curtains and shades are explained in the chapter on basic techniques (see pp. 38–57), from how to measure your window and estimate how much fabric to buy, to how to put up a pole and make a hand-pleated heading. This section provides all the backup information you need as you work through the projects.

The projects (see pp. 60–123) cover a range of curtain and shade styles from the very simple to the more ornate, each featuring a different technique. Clear step-by-step instructions guide you through the process of making these beautiful window furnishings and cross references to the basic techniques help you find all the help you need.

I hope the projects and other ideas I have included in this book encourage you to make your own innovative and professional-looking curtains and shades. Once you start, you will be amazed at how easy it is to transform your windows. Be inspired and start sewing!

Melanie Paine 1997

ASSESSING WINDOWS

Windows function as providers of light, as architectural detail, and as frames through which you view the outside world. They are important features in a room and you should take into account their various functions when choosing how to dress them. Therefore, before deciding on a style of curtain or shade, first consider the shape and proportions of your window in relation to the rest of the room and whether its position in the room poses any limitations on the type of window treatments you can use.

Most windows fall into one of these categories: portrait (taller than wide), landscape (wider than high), or square. There can of course be multiples of these, and in some cases two or more portrait windows that are side by side in a wall may become a landscape shape. Portrait windows are the most common shape and the most versatile in

Pair of identical windows in same wall

These should be treated as one or in the same way. You could opt for two pairs of curtains, two shades, or one single curtain on each window, mirroring one another (see p. 86).

Two different windows in same wall

Whether you use curtains or shades, give smaller, lower-height windows a heading at the same level as their larger neighbor. Consider the decorative impact when curtains are open and windows revealed, as well as when they are closed.

Two or more different windows in the same room

In this situation it pays to choose different arrangements for the different window styles, but to stick to the same fabrics. If, for example, one pair of curtains has a contrast border, then use the same idea on a neighboring shade. You can also link the two by using the same style poles or tiebacks.

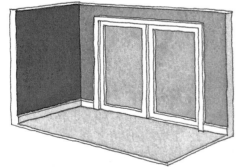

Window or sliding door taking up all or most of a wall

Here, you need to think carefully about where the curtains will hang when the window or door is open. Often there is little room to either side of the window, therefore avoid thick fabrics or heavily gathered headings that will cause the fabric to bulk.

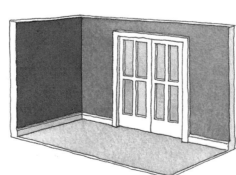

French doors

These lend themselves to a pair of curtains hanging down both sides. There may be some restrictions if the doors open inward, so position poles wisely. Keep curtaining simple and hold curtains off the windows with tiebacks to provide clear access.

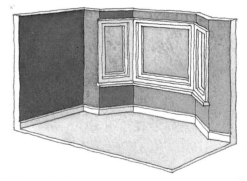

Bay window

The normal way to treat a bay window is with a curved track concealed with some kind of pelmet or fascia (see p. 76). However, you could treat each window singly, with Roman or panel shades, for example.

terms of how they can be dressed. They are often set high in the wall and can extend to the floor as with French doors (see opposite). Portrait windows can take a pair of curtains in any style, most forms of shade, or a single curtain, perhaps extended to the floor to accentuate the shape and held with a tie-back on one side.

Landscape windows range from large picture windows and sliding doors to side-by-side loft windows and small casements. Pairs of curtains in most styles suit this category. However, keep your headings relatively simple to avoid making the window appear squat and top heavy. Where windows are very wide, curtaining can be difficult as there is so much fabric to "store" at each side. Consider shades for a simpler, less cluttered feel.

Square windows can be tiny cottage windows, often recessed, or much larger windows that are often found in more contemporary homes. For the former you need a treatment that does not need much space around the window, while for the latter you need one that lets in the maximum light during the day.

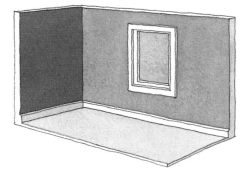

Single window in a wall
Here, you have almost carte blanche. Whichever style you choose, remain close to the proportions of the window. Instead of a pair of curtains, you could balance a single curtain with furniture or pictures, or hang a shade.

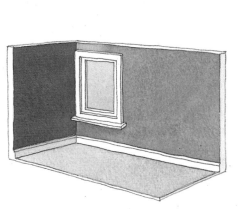

Window close to an adjacent wall
Partitioning a room often results in an off-center window. Emphasize this asymmetry and go for a single curtain with a strongly decorative heading and chunky tieback (see p. 64).

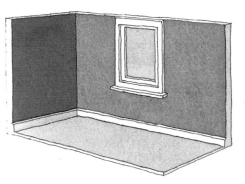

Window close to a ceiling
If there is no wall space for a support, you can use a ceiling fixing, or fix a fabric-covered board securely to the ceiling to spread the weight of a pole or track beneath it.

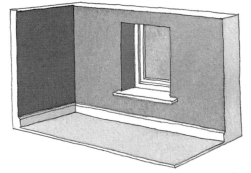

Window in a deep recess
This requires simple window furnishings – slot-head curtains on slim poles or those that can swing out from their fixings. If light is important, avoid bulky fabrics that will block the window. Fix poles close to the window and into the frame.

Window with radiator beneath
This problem is best treated with a simple design solution such as a sill-length curtain or shade. Or, ignore the radiator and go for floor-length curtains. Try, for example, a single curtain on a pole pulled back to one side and balanced with a chunky rope looped around the curtainless end of the pole.

Window on stairs, where floor is uneven
Shades are ideal for this situation, but you could consider a single curtain, embellished with wonderful tiebacks or ornate finials.

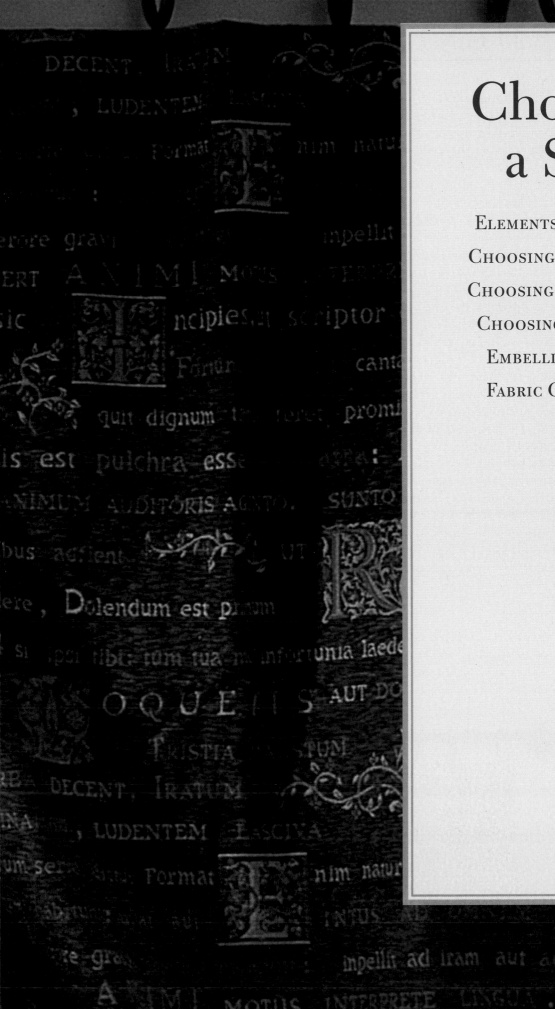

Choosing a Style

ELEMENTS OF STYLE

WITH CURTAINS AND SHADES, there are a number of different elements that combine together to influence the overall look, and you can use each one to add style and interest to your window treatment.

The most important element is the fabric you choose, whether it be a delicate muslin or voile for a light and airy effect, rich and inviting velvet or tapestry for a warm, sumptuous feel, or boldly patterned and brightly colored fabric for a look that will dominate a room. Consider the texture and weight of the fabric as well as its color and pattern, and decide whether you want the curtain or shade to blend in with the rest of the decoration or to stand out as a feature.

The support you choose will also influence the finished look of your curtain or, to a lesser extent, shade. First decide whether you want wall, window frame, or ceiling attachments. Curtain poles come in many different styles and are often a decorative feature in their own right, especially when you combine them with rings and finials. Alternatively, use track, either left uncovered or hidden with a lath and fascia, a pelmet, or a drape hung from a pole above. With certain types of shade you can use a pole, but generally a shade is attached to a lath.

A separate, but closely linked element, is your choice of heading. This controls the way your curtains hang, so use the heading positively to reinforce the style you have chosen. If you want a simple effect, with the fabric falling as a flat panel when the curtain is pulled across, try a slot heading around a pole or a series of hand-sewn hooks attached to rings. Alternatively, for a richer effect, gather the curtains with tape for extra fullness or sew them into more elaborate pleats. This will make a special feature of the heading and allow the fabric to drape and fold in different ways all the way down its length. Although the fabric of most shades falls as a flat panel from the lath or pole, you can introduce pleats that run from top to bottom and are accentuated when the shade is pulled up.

Finally, you can further influence the style of your windows by adding embellishments. Combine their practical purposes – tiebacks that keep curtains off the window or ties that hold up simple panel shades – with their decorative potential. Embellishments add texture and definition to your window treatment – from simple piping to contrast border panels and fringing.

You can use each of these features to influence the overall design and add a personalized touch to your decor. Try some unexpected combinations, such as complementing a grand fabric with a simple wooden pole and hand-sewn hooks, or using a simple fabric with a grand goblet-pleat heading and braid border, while holding it off the window with a tasseled tieback. Also remember that there is a degree of interdependence between the different elements; your choice of fabric will be limited by the maximum weight that the support can take, while the way a fabric hangs and the type of pattern it has should influence the type of heading you choose.

SUPPORT

When choosing your support (see pp. 14–17), consider both its aesthetic appeal and the characteristics of the window. Look at the amount of space available for attaching a support, as well as the weight of the fabric it must hold.

HEADING

Headings (see pp. 18–19) provide decoration at the top of your curtain or shade and control how the fabric hangs down its length. You can use them to emphasize a grand design or give an extra touch to a simple curtain.

An unusual solution
This treatment demonstrates how the different elements of style work together. In this unusual situation, curtains are hung halfway up huge windows. The simple wire support is almost invisible, leaving the view through the windows unimpeded when the curtains are pulled back. The heading – a row of eyelets punched along the top of the curtain – is in keeping with the support, and the curtains are, by necessity, unlined and made of a light fabric so that the wire can support them.

FABRIC

The type of fabric (see pp. 20–27) you choose will assert greatest influence on your decor. Whether you prefer heavy or light, warm or cool, or subtle or striking fabrics, make sure that your heading suits your fabric and that the support is strong enough to hold its weight.

EMBELLISHMENT

Use embellishments – ties, tassels, braids, fringes – (see pp. 28–31) both for practical purposes, such as holding back a curtain or holding up a shade, and for adding extra texture and definition to the edges of your window treatment.

CHOOSING A SUPPORT

FOR CURTAINS, poles are the most attractive kind of support (see pp. 16–17 for details on the many varieties of poles and their accessories). They are attached to the wall, window frame, or the ceiling with brackets (see p. 52). The curtain is supported on rings and, as both pole and rings are visible, can contribute greatly to the overall style of your window treatment.

The other option is to use track, which is functional rather than decorative. It can be left uncovered but is more often covered with fabric. The simplest type of track consists of a lath and fascia. The lath is a piece of wood fitted at right angles to the wall or window frame and supported by an angle bracket. The fascia, a slim piece of plywood, is fixed to its front to hide the track.

POLE

The simplest types of poles rest in a bracket that is fixed to a wall. Small screws at the front of the bracket are screwed into the pole once it is in place to secure it (see p. 52 for instructions on putting up a pole).

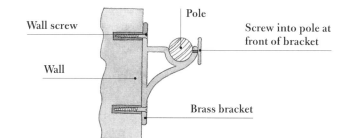

Wall screw   Pole   Screw into pole at front of bracket

Wall   Brass bracket

UNCOVERED TRACK

Tracks are available in plastic and metal, but metal is better because it is stronger. For best results, order track from a professional who can also install it, especially if it needs to be curved. If you do it yourself, follow instructions provided with the track, since they vary from brand to brand (see also p. 53).

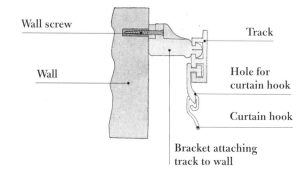

Wall screw   Track

Wall   Hole for curtain hook

Curtain hook

Bracket attaching track to wall

Ceiling-fitted pole
This brass pole supports a straightforward curtain arrangement. The pole is suspended from long brackets fitted on chunky ceiling beams. It is always easier to fit pole brackets into wood rather than walls and a ceiling fixing is sometimes the answer.

Invisible track
Tracks are generally covered, but in some situations a simple thin white metal or plastic track "disappears" against a window frame or into the top of a recess. In this example, the track is hardly visible and does not detract from the curtains' look.

Some tracks are already corded when purchased. This is especially good if you intend to hang light-colored or delicate fabrics, because the curtains do not have to be handled when pulled across the window. You can use them when there is not enough room between window and ceiling for a pole, and you can bend them to fit the angles of a bay or the curves of a bow window. This is not easy, however, and is best done by a professional.

Whether you use a pole or track, remember that heavy or full-length curtains always need substantial support and that any installation is only as strong as the surface to which it is attached. If a wall is too soft or uneven, brackets should be fitted into the window frame, which is likely to be stronger. Avoid using ceiling tracks unless there are wooden beams that can support the brackets.

Your choice of support for shades is far simpler. You can hang some styles of shade from a pole if they have a slot heading or attach them with café clips (see p. 17). But, generally, shades are hung from a lath attached to the wall with brackets. If there is no room for the brackets, or if you want to hang a shade in front of a recess, you can attach the lath to the ceiling with a screw.

COVERED TRACK

You can hide track with a lath and fascia. The lath, a 2 x 1-in (5 x 2.5-cm) piece of wood, is fitted at right angles to the wall and the fascia, a slim piece of plywood, fixed to its front (see pp. 56–57 for how to put up laths). The track is fixed to the lath's underside, and the fascia is deep enough to hide the track while allowing the runners to move freely.

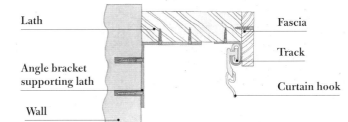

Lath — Fascia — Track — Angle bracket supporting lath — Curtain hook — Wall

LATH FOR SHADE

A wooden lath to support a shade is fixed to the ceiling with screws or supported on angle brackets that are screwed to the wall. The lath itself is covered in fabric to match the shade, making a discreet fixing (see pp. 55–57 for instructions on covering and securing laths).

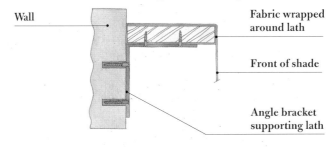

Wall — Fabric wrapped around lath — Front of shade — Angle bracket supporting lath

Using a lath and fascia
The track that supports these curtains is hidden by a lath and fascia covered in the same fabric as the curtains. A track was a good choice here since there is little space above the doors to fit a pole.

Shade on a lath
One of the advantages of using a lath is that it is hidden. The shade appears simply as a panel of fabric unencumbered by brackets and poles. In this example, the lath is supported by angle brackets that are attached to the window frame.

Poles and accessories

Wrought iron rod and finial in one

Chrome rod with matching finial

Dark wood pole with matching finial

Painted wood pole with matching finial

Thick brass pole with decorative finial

Thin brass pole with fleur-de-lis finial

Poles come in a wide range of materials and finishes, including polished or painted wood, brushed nickel, antique brass, or wrought iron. They can be fun or formal, handmade or mass-produced, carved and gilded, or even pasted in wallpaper.

Poles are supported on chunky wooden brackets or on slender brass versions. For poles that have to be fitted into a recess or against an adjacent wall there are special brackets that encase the end of the pole. These are available in wood or brass to match the pole.

Finials are the ornaments fitted onto each end of the pole, or to one end if the pole abuts a wall. They perform the practical task of stopping the last curtain ring from

Poles

Give as much thought to choosing the style of pole and finial as to the curtain or shade itself. Try mixing brass and wood together or contrasting different colors of wood. If you are using a beautiful pole, make sure that the style of curtain allows it to be seen to full advantage.

Finials

Many poles come with matching finials and some have finials that are actually a part of the pole. Others can be fitted to any pole and give you a chance to experiment with different combinations. Try teaming an ornate pole with simple finials or dress up a plain pole with the wildest finials you can find.

RINGS

Brass ring **Wooden ring** **Iron ring** **Painted ring**

falling off the rod, but they are also decorative elements in their own right and often provide a window treatment with a much needed finishing touch.

Attaching your curtain or shade

Rings are the most common form of attachment for curtains, and most poles come with matching rings. Despite this, experiment with different combinations of pole and ring if you feel so inclined – just remember that the rings need to be at least ½ in (1.25 cm) larger in diameter than the pole.

As an alternative to rings, chrome or brass eyelets punched through the top of the curtain make a strong decorative device. Whether they are made from the same fabric as the main curtain or from a contrasting color or pattern, tapes, ribbon ties, or fabric tabs sewn at intervals across the top of a curtain also look pretty. In the case of fabric tabs, loop them over the pole and fasten them to the curtain with a button or stud.

You can stitch a slot at the top of your curtain or shade and then simply thread a pole into it. The pole is then hidden, apart from the finials at either end.

A similar option is to use clips that grip the top of the curtain or shade and encircle the pole. They are available in a variety of finishes, from brass or bronze to painted metal. If you choose to create a slot or use clips for curtains, remember that you will not be able to draw them back. For this reason, they generally work best with lightweight fabrics that do not block out all of the daylight.

Twisted wire
These interestingly shaped pieces of wire act as both rings and hooks. They are set off by the simplicity of the bare metal pole and eyelet heading.

OTHER ATTACHMENTS

Eyelet and rope   **Tie**   **Tab and button**   **Café clip**

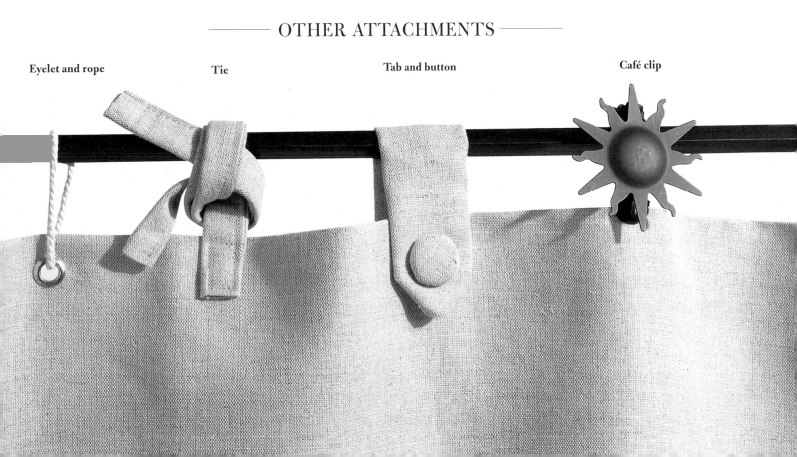

CHOOSING A HEADING

THE HEADING RUNS horizontally across the top of the window treatment and controls the way the fabric hangs. With curtains, there is normally some fullness in their width – more fabric than window width – and how the fabric is pulled up into the finished width is determined by the type of heading used.

At its most basic, the heading can make the fabric hang as a flat panel with hardly any fullness. You can achieve this by using a slot heading, or by sewing hooks or ties on to the curtain and attaching it to rings on a pole.

For a gathered heading you can sew curtain tape to the top of the curtain at the back when it is flat. Strings that

Formal pleats
Smart, cream-colored curtains with a French, or pinch, pleat heading are ideal for this simple, yet sophisticated room. The groups of pleats, spaced at regular intervals across the top of the curtain hold the fabric in neatly disciplined folds. They can be used with tracks or poles.

Slot heading
Simple to make (see p. 48), this works best for shades and short, lightweight curtains that don't need to be pulled across.

Goblet pleats
An impressive formal heading (see p. 51), it is good for long curtains and is often used with rich, heavy fabrics.

Gathered heading
Use 1-in (2.5-cm) tape for a simple gathered heading (see p. 49). It is suitable for both small, casual curtains and long, full curtains.

Box pleats
Box pleats provide a neat, structured look (see p. 51). They work particularly well with crisp, thin fabrics as opposed to bulkier ones.

run through the tape are then pulled until the curtain is reduced to the required width. The two most common tapes are 1-in (2.5-cm) tape, which gives a simple gathered heading and is usually set down from the top of the curtain to make a "stand-up" heading above the tape, and 3-in (7.5-cm) tape, which creates deep pencil pleats, producing multiple folds in the fabric.

There are also tapes available for making French, box, and even goblet pleats, but it is better if you do these by hand since they will look and hang much better. This is especially true when you are hanging your curtain from a pole since the heading will be visible.

When choosing your curtain heading, make sure that it is suitable for the fabric and appropriate for the setting. Bleached canvas on the windows of a loft apartment would look odd arranged in neat French pleats. A heavy classical brocade would not work with a narrow slot heading. But don't be afraid to experiment and discover unpredictable combinations. Taffeta silk could look splendid with a heading of chunky eyelets, or try rich velvet curtains with brightly colored tab headings.

For shades, there is not the same degree of choice as with curtains. Whether a pole or lath is used to support the shade, the fabric simply hangs down from the top like a flat panel. Any folds or pleats in a shade do not rely so much on the heading as on the way in which the shade is raised. Depending on the type of cording system used (see p. 54), the shade will bunch or fold in different ways when it is pulled up, and some will form delicate scooped shapes along the bottom.

Simple slot heading

Two parallel lines of stitching through doubled fabric at the top of this curtain make a simple sleeve, or slot, through which the pole is threaded. Slot-headed curtains can only be partially opened. When closed, the fabric can fall as a flat panel or, if the curtain has more fullness as shown here, take on a gathered appearance.

Pencil pleats
Created with 3-in (7.5-cm) tape, the fabric is gathered into tight pleats (see p. 48). This heading is best used beneath pelmets or drapes.

Hand-sewn hooks
These hooks (see p. 49) work with most fabrics and give a simple, ungathered look. They can be visible, as here, or hidden behind the top of the curtain or shade.

French pleats
A formal heading, this is made of groups of three pleats (see p. 50). The style is most suitable for long, floor-length curtains.

Eyelets
Easy to make with a punch and dye kit (see p. 49), eyelets create an attractive, informal effect on curtains or shades.

CHOOSING A FABRIC

Light or heavy

THE COLOR AND TEXTURE of a fabric determines its style and the effect it has on a room. Light fabrics may look frivolous, while heavy fabrics may appear more serious and grand. A richly patterned tapestry, for example, is weighty and usually comes in traditional dark colors. Curtains in such a fabric would rightly dominate a room, and accessories as well as other furnishings should be of equal stature. At the other end of the scale, fine, beautiful pale silks or linens lend an airiness that the rest of the room should follow. Pale, neutral colors on walls and other furnishings would extend the feeling of lightness. But equally, a rich dark red wall would accentuate the fragility and beauty of such light fabrics.

Woven fabrics, particularly those with textured embellishments, such as brocade, are among some of the heaviest. Wool, which is one of the heaviest fibers, produces some of the heaviest fabrics. But cotton, too, can be heavy if the weave structure is dense. Flimsy, loosely woven cottons, such as lace or muslin, however, are feather light. Silk is generally finely woven and makes a light fabric. Heavy, richly textured fabrics, such as tapestry and damask, need to be anchored with strong fabrics on cushions or throws and should fit the overall decor of

Light and airy
Graceful folds of white muslin cover the whole of this ceiling-to-floor and wall-to-wall window. The curtains protect the room from the direct rays of the sun, yet still allow it to be bathed in light, giving an airy feel.

LIGHT FABRICS

The delicate floral pattern on this cotton fabric gives it a gentle appearance.

The ground color of this cotton stripe lightens its appearance. It would work both on its own and as a lining for heavier fabrics.

A painted silver pattern swirls across the surface of this cotton fabric, giving it a light, graceful look.

A delicate lacy fabric with a leaf motif, this has an open weave that allows light to shine through.

The pale background pattern adds a subtle lightness to this cotton floral print.

the room. Use chunky wooden or painted finials or old brass pelmets as embellishments, and add heavy tassels or fringes to edges. Heavy fabrics need sturdy support, so make sure that the wall or window frame is strong enough to hold a weighty pole or track.

Points to note

• Sheer and open-weave fabrics, such as muslin and lace, allow plenty of light into a room and protect other furnishings from direct sunlight. Use sheers on their own on a window or with heavier main curtains or shades.

• Lace is often made in a panel with one central design and side borders. To look their best, these panels should be hung, without fullness, from a slim pole or rod. For an attractive, light-diffusing effect, back open-weave fabrics, such as lace and voile, with a colored lining.

• A heavy fabric is warmer, excludes light, and keeps out drafts. Some heavy fabrics, such as tapestry and thick wool chenille, are bulky and their weave makes them stiff. These fabrics are wonderful for panel shades that roll up or for flatter styles of curtain. They do not drape or pleat easily, so do not use them for curtains with headings that rely on tight pleating or neat folds. Velvet, on the other hand, is fluid despite its thickness and works well with pleated headings.

Heavy and opulent
The weighty printed cotton curtains and tapestry shade combine to give a look of warmth and sumptuousness. They are ideal for a bedroom as they would block out even the brightest dawn and provide a cozy atmosphere on cold winter nights.

HEAVY FABRICS

A heavy tapestry fabric woven as a 12-in (30-cm) strip works well as an edging for plain fabrics.

The ribbed surface of this patterned and striped cotton adds stiffness. It can be used for borders or for curtains or shades.

This rich brocade in traditional colors drapes beautifully, despite its weight, and makes excellent curtains.

The surface of this thick, gold-patterned wool is slightly raised. The fabric is reversible.

A dramatic weighty silk damask, this needs to be used on a large scale to show its pattern to full effect.

Plain or patterned

Both plain and patterned fabrics come in a wide variety of styles. With plain fabrics, texture is all important since there is no pattern or mix of colors to obscure it. Think of velvet, hessian, silk, or roughly textured cotton – each has its own particular surface, which is what gives it character and alters the way light interacts with the cloth. Natural fabrics, such as cotton, give a simple, fresh look; wool and velvet bring warmth to a room and can also add a degree of grandeur; while silk possesses a refined, elegant

quality. With pattern, it is the design and the scale of the design that set the tone. Floral motifs add an informal, country touch to a room, while a bold stripe always introduces a sense of elegant classicism.

Harmony and contrast

When choosing your fabric always consider the other decoration in the room first. Plain fabrics can work well with plain colored walls and floors to create a minimalist look. But if you find a lack of contrast monotonous, you could add a patterned wall or break it up with pictures.

When using patterned fabrics the key is always to achieve the right balance. Use patterned fabric with plain and make the colors harmonize or contrast, depending on the visual effect you want to achieve. A dark brown border will soften the effect of a dazzling black and white patterned curtain. You can even mix pattern with pattern, provided that there is a strong color link between the two. An edging in a busy floral print, for example, adds pattern to a strong stripe. When mixing patterns it is crucial to make it clear where one begins and another ends or the result is likely to be a muddled mess.

Natural simplicity
Bleached cream surfaces harmonize beneath a flood of natural light to create an atmosphere of simplicity and calm in this elegant interior. The stark geometry of the window panes is offset by the plain, neutral fabrics used for the furniture and shades. The effect is one of light and shadow, form, and shape.

PLAIN FABRICS

This robust red cotton twill is plain, in that it is all one color, but strongly textured. It drapes very well.	More mat than gloss, the surface of this plain green velvet catches just enough light to give it richness.	A woven motif, with raised and flat areas, creates an overall pattern so subtle that the silk damask appears plain.	This chenille has a tiny gold motif, which gives it character. It drapes beautifully and makes good borders.	From a distance, this fabric appears to be plain and all one color, but the tiny check adds interest close up.

Points to note

• When using plain or subtly patterned fabrics, you need to consider carefully the properties of the fabric that you choose. As there is no pattern to distract the eye, the texture of the fabric and the way that it folds and hangs becomes crucial.

• When using plain fabric on a large window, avoid using primary or near primary colors – a broad expanse of just one color might be overpowering.

• Do not use fabric with a large pattern on a small window since there will not be enough space to see the whole design. Conversely, if you use a fabric with a small pattern on a large window, be aware that from a distance the pattern disappears and the fabric appears as one color.

• Choose your heading with care when using patterned fabrics; elaborate pleats could obscure the pattern. As a general rule, the more ornate the pattern, the simpler the heading should be.

Casual gingham

The relaxed country style of this kitchen is complemented by the classically simple blue and white check used for these curtains. For added harmony, the same fabric was used for the pillow on the chair.

PATTERNED FABRICS

A variation on the French toile de Jouy, this is a beautifully printed cotton with many soft colors.

This striking motif, on a thick, heavy cotton fabric, would stand out in any decorating scheme.

A dramatic printed cotton with architectural motifs, this is best used flat to give the pattern its full impact.

With its lively overall pattern, this chintz can be used flat or gathered into curtains. It drapes well.

Classic club stripes add a touch of distinction to any room. Woven in wool, this rich fabric has a subtle line of yellow.

Warm or cool

Color is the most important factor in determining whether a fabric looks warm or cool. There are of course "warm" blues and "cool" reds, but a blue and white stripe will generally look and feel cooler than a red and white stripe. However, texture also plays a part. Some blues look warmer in a woven mat fabric, while a glazed fabric can appear cool even when in a bright color.

Earthy colors, such as ochre, terra-cotta, olive green, and burgundy give a feeling of warmth and coziness. Easy on the eye, they are undemanding in terms of other furnishings and decoration. Acid yellows and sharp greens are cooler and more dominant. They need careful balancing and are best used in a quality cloth.

Color combinations

Colors, when combined, affect one another. A stripe of navy blue will cool a vibrant scarlet curtain, but add turquoise or cobalt blue instead, and the scarlet becomes even more dramatic. Strong lime green and indigo are both cool colors but can look hot if used together – despite the old adage "blue and green should never be seen."

When combining colors, balance is the key to success. Flamboyant color combinations can look stunning but they need careful consideration or they may become a confusing muddle. Use strident colors in smaller areas for

Warm exuberance
Warmth and richness exude from every surface in this beautifully decorated interior. Intense reds, golds, and warm ochres dominate and, although they are balanced by the cooler colors in the carpet, create an exuberant atmosphere. The red of the dramatic curtain arrangement, which is definitely at the hot end of the color spectrum, is intensified by the natural light streaming through the window.

WARM FABRICS

Ochre and terra-cotta, both warm earthy colors, combine in this woven ribbed cotton.

A pale coffee-colored background softens the rich reds and yellows in this exuberantly designed chintz.

A deep rust-red background gives this paisley-patterned cotton print a warm look.

Rich colors and a soft texture combine to give a warm feel to this woven brocade.

The buttercup yellow of this woolen damask creates a warm sunny glow.

the best effect. A bright panel of warm primary color on a curtain or shade hung in a room decorated in black and white would be dramatic.

Try making interesting pairs of colors – warm yellow with cool navy; pale coffee with rich burgundy. Color can also enable you to link different fabrics. A rich heavy velvet can work well with a shiny checked taffeta if there is a color in common. Even the tiniest thread of color can join two or more completely different fabrics into a workable partnership.

Try making a scrapbook of samples of different types of fabrics; it will help you to create unexpected and interesting combinations. Remember, though, that colors that look wonderful on a small scale might not work well when spread over a large area.

Points to note

• If sharp white laces and linens appear too cool, soften the effect with honey-colored jute tiebacks and a rich red mahogany pole.
• Warm up cool dark rooms with an array of fiery colors that reflect light and add zing.
• Some colors, such as citrus lime and lemon, can be hot or cool. The colors in the rest of the room affect how they appear in any decorative situation.
• Fabrics influence the surfaces that surround them. Crisp white cotton with white washed walls and a stone floor make a room look and feel cool. If a cream fabric is used instead of brilliant white, the rest of the room will be subtly warmed.
• Fabrics are affected by the light in a room. Natural light and electric light change the way a fabric looks, so bear this in mind when making your choice.

Cool checks
Sparklingly fresh, this crisp blue and white fabric sweeps across bright bay windows, keeping out the sun and lowering the temperature. A plain blue border at the top continues the cool theme and helps to define the shape of the window.

COOL FABRICS

This cool, crisp poplin drapes beautifully and also looks good as a pleated or rolled shade.

A classic blue and white plaid, this cotton check can be used for any type of curtain, shade, or border.

These blue tulips printed on silk would be best shown off on floor-length curtains with a simple gathered heading.

This inky-blue velvet drapes in thick folds and is excellent for heavy curtains.

A crisp cotton with a cool blue and red pattern works well for flat curtains or pleated shades.

Subtle or striking

Subtle fabrics, with their quiet elegance, usually blend comfortably with their surroundings. Using fabrics with subtle patterns or colors, however, requires careful thought. A mix of whites, off-whites, and pale coffee fabrics in one curtain arrangement could look lovely, provided the rest of the decor is also subtle and does not distract. White on white, or close to white, patterns look handsome and can be combined with other subtle fabrics.

For example, try making a shade in white cotton with a small motif in cream, border it with a pale coffee and white stripe, and hang it from a scrubbed white pole. Minimal color combinations in interesting textures can produce restful, but beautiful results.

Other fabrics that dazzle and shock can offer a room dramatic charm. Imagine a single window with a flourish of pink velvet around its frame in a white room with

Subtle serenity
Balance and symmetry, achieved by a quiet but clever use of color and form, are the key elements in this interior. The window furnishings blend with the walls. The shades are functional but do not make a strong decorative statement. Instead they are a subtle part of the room's architecture.

SUBTLE FABRICS

Muted grays and blues combine with a red and ochre plaid in this soft woolen tweed.

This lightweight sheer cotton fabric has a barely visible thin stripe woven through it.

A small square motif gives this heavy white cotton fabric subtle pattern and texture.

The two colors in this woven fabric are close in tone, giving the impression of subtle pattern.

This classic black and cream ticking is in a soft cotton that drapes well.

stripped floorboards. The setting allows such a fabric to stand out and calls attention to its drama.

Many striking fabrics have bold color combinations – bright orange against aquamarine with a dash of raspberry pink, for example. Use this kind of fabric for a plain shade, or for a curtain with a simple heading of hand-sewn hooks or clips. Contrasting surfaces and texture as well as color can also produce striking combinations within a shade or set of curtains. Try using shiny, bright fabrics alongside those with a mat surface.

Points to note

• A strong color or dramatic pattern can be balanced by a more soothing, subtle palette. One should attractively enhance the other, but avoid too obvious clashes where the combination of subtle touches and drama is overdone.

• Avoid using large, striking designs on small windows as the intended dramatic effect may be lost.

• When planning to decorate a room with dramatic fabrics that have a potentially dominant image or pattern, try to select from large fabric samples. Hold them up at the window, if possible, so that their color or pattern or both may be read from a distance. Often what you see on a tiny scrap of fabric changes completely when scaled up.

• When working on adjacent rooms, the decoration and furnishing should be considered together. This is especially so with rooms that open off halls or landings, for example, where the relationship between subtle or striking is paramount.

• To achieve a dramatic effect you need to be able to see and "read" the fabric clearly. Striking fabrics have the strength to stand on their own. They do not need complicated arrangements, which only lessen their effect.

• You can use a mixture of bold, strong patterns if color links the different fabrics and the overall arrangement is kept fairly simple.

Bold tartan
The shape of this room and the position of its windows make it a challenge to curtain. A suitably dramatic fabric, this bold, predominantly red tartan makes a wide sweep of strong color and pattern.

STRIKING FABRICS

The boldness of this wool tartan in strident colors is its strength, and it should be used flamboyantly.

A figured velvet in rich luscious colors, this fabric shimmers as the light catches its surface.

With its striking pattern on a black ground, this heavy cotton weave needs to be used in dramatic surroundings.

An Indian cotton, woven in an unusual color combination, would make bold curtains or shades.

The vivid contrasting stripes of this cotton print can be used horizontally or vertically to make flat shades.

EMBELLISHMENTS

FRINGES, BRAIDS, tassels, buttons, and other kinds of embellishments are all ways to add interest to curtains and shades. Purely decorative, they provide contrasting color and texture. They are usually applied around the edges of a curtain or shade by hand and help to define its shape. The addition of a navy blue chenille fringe along the leading edge of a curtain in pale cream silk, for example, lifts the arrangement and gives the eye a line to follow when the curtain is pulled back.

There are many ways to use such embellishments. Hand-sew plain flat braids to the edges of Roman shades before the fabric is made up. Or add flat fabric borders in contrasting fabrics or colors to the edges of curtains or shades, again defining shape and adding additional color or texture. These borders, sewn to the fabric before it is made up, can be added to the perimeter or inset in the main fabric and be made from one piece or alternate colors. Adding borders is also a good way of mixing different textures of fabric together. Consider combining a rough hessian with a simple flat cotton, both in the same color.

Cord or rope made from cotton or silks, or a combination of both, can define the edge of a curtain. Hand-sewn to the finished curtain along the leading edge or across the heading, it is a subtle way of adding texture.

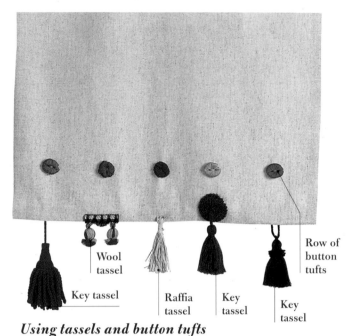

Wool tassel

Row of button tufts

Key tassel

Raffia tassel

Key tassel

Key tassel

Using tassels and button tufts

You can embellish the base of a shade with a row of button tufts running along several inches (centimeters) above the bottom edge or with tassels hanging down from it. Use small chunky key tassels in cotton, wool, and raffia, or simple mattress tufts.

Embellishing the edges of curtains

A border, piping, or fringe down the edge of a curtain should look as though it belongs to the fabric it decorates. Color should relate to the fabric or to a nearby decorative element in the room. Here, the curtain fringe coordinates perfectly with the silk fabric of the curtains and lends weight and texture.

Using fringes and borders
To give added definition, color, and texture to the base of a shade, you can hand-sew on a fringe. If your main fabric is neutral, try jazzing it up with a contrasting border, such as a striking strip of tapestry (see above).

—— EMBELLISHING THE TOP OF A CURTAIN ——

Self-pelmet
To give extra interest to the heading of a curtain, add a border to the front so that it adorns the top of the curtain like a pelmet. You can use a completely different fabric, as shown here, but there should be a color link between the two.

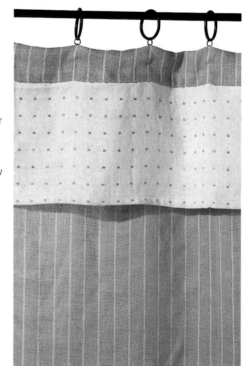

Soft drape
Another way of embellishing the top of a curtain is with a drape of fabric that hangs from a pole above the curtain and hides the curtain's heading. The drape pictured here, with its dark red horizontal stripe, adds a dash of bold color to the simple calico curtain hanging beneath it.

Using tiebacks

Tiebacks are both decorative and practical. They hold the curtain back from the window to allow in as much light as possible, but they also shape the curtain into graceful folds. Generally, a tieback loops around a concealed hook fixed into the wall next to the window.

Rope and tassel tiebacks are available ready-made. Better still, make your own from a variety of different materials. Silk and lengths of tapestry fabric make beautiful tiebacks, but simple jute also looks extremely effective. Add tassels to lengths of jute or plait several lengths together. Lengths of ribbon or braid, with rings sewn at each end for looping over the hook, or tied for more casual effect, work well and are easily changed to give a new look. For full-length curtains, fix tiebacks at roughly one-third the length of the curtain from the floor. However, if you are using long tassels, place the hooks farther up so that the tassels hang correctly against the curtain.

Alternatively, you can use holdbacks made of wood, brass, or other metal. Simply fix the holdback to the wall so that the curtain can be looped behind it, making sure that the back edge of the curtain remains vertical. This arrangement generally only works when the curtain hangs just past each side of the window and the holdback is fitted close to the frame or window edge. Rosettes, in brass or wood, may also be used as glorified hooks for holding rope tiebacks.

You cannot use a tieback with shades, but in much the same way as you use a tieback to hold back a curtain, you can use a tie to hold up a simple panel shade (see p. 100).

Seashell tieback
Rows of tiny white cowrie shells make an unusual but attractive tieback. They coordinate well with the pattern of the border fabric and add texture to the curtain. The shiny surface of the shells catches the light.

TRADITIONAL TIEBACKS

Single-tassel jute tieback attached to wall

Double-tassel jute tieback attached to wall

Silk and cotton tieback attached to wall

Jute plait attached to wall

POSITIONING TIEBACKS

The position of the tieback affects the way a curtain hangs.
The three main ways of placing tiebacks are shown below, but you
can experiment by trying one in different positions until the
curtain makes a shape that you like.

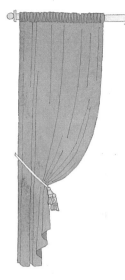

Around the pole

Looping a tieback around the curtain and over the pole gathers the fabric and brings the curtain's leading edge off the ground. This arrangement is best used where the curtain is not often moved.

Center of the curtain

You can position a tieback around the center of the curtain, part of the way down its length. The supporting hook is behind the curtain. Pull the curtain out above the tieback to give it shape.

Low down the curtain

Tiebacks positioned low on the curtain and fixed to the side of it should generally be set two thirds of the way down. If, however, you are using long tassels, lift the tieback higher.

ALTERNATIVE TIEBACKS

Rope twisted around
drape and tied

Tapestry band
around drape

Brass hook
attached to wall

Brass rosette
attached to wall

FABRIC GLOSSARY

THE NATURAL RAW MATERIALS that make up furnishing fabrics are cotton, linen, wool, and silk. Each has its own characteristics and there are many variations within each type. In addition to these, there are humanmade fibers, some of which are combined with natural materials to produce a blend. All fabrics, with the exception of one or two, such as felt, are woven. They are produced on looms and usually consist of weft threads (those that travel from side to side) and warp threads (those that travel up and down).

While some types of fabric are best for certain situations – flimsy muslin for privacy and light diffusion, tapestry for insulation – there are no hard and fast rules for choosing fabric for your windows. Shown here is a selection ranging from linings and basic fabrics through neutrals to colored fabrics. Browse and be inspired.

Linings and basic fabrics

Interlining (thick)
This is made of combed cotton and comes in a variety of thicknesses. It is placed between fabric and lining in curtains to provide insulation as well as body and weight.

Lining
Standard lining is made of a tightly woven cotton fabric called sateen. This keeps its shape well, even after dry cleaning. Lining is generally used in cream or white, but it is also available in a range of colors.

Thermal lining
This is standard cotton lining that is coated with a layer of aluminum on one side for insulation. The coated side is silver-gray and should lie against the fabric. The other side is usually a light color.

Blackout lining
This is made up of one layer of opaque material between two layers of cotton lining fabric. It blocks out all light and is best used with solid, opaque fabrics rather than those whose appeal depends on their translucency.

Calico
An inexpensive fabric, calico is raw unbleached cotton with a plain weave. It was originally used as a lining and backing fabric, but it is now popular for all kinds of window dressings.

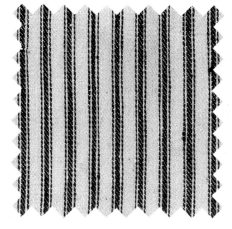

Black and white ticking
A strong, tightly woven cotton, this is based on the fabric traditionally used to cover mattresses. This version is softer and less dense than mattress ticking, so it drapes easily.

Neutral and simply patterned fabrics

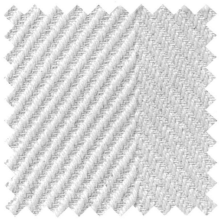

Herringbone cotton

A diagonally patterned, or herringbone, weave gives this heavy cotton its chunky texture. Strong and hard-wearing, it is a good choice for thick curtains.

French ticking

This closely woven cotton fabric is based on the traditional striped material used to cover mattresses. It is suitable for all kinds of window furnishings.

Cotton with open grid

Lightweight and almost sheer, this cotton fabric has a pattern of open gridwork embroidery across its surface. It works well for full curtains that do not need to exclude light.

Printed muslin

Muslin is a fine, translucent cotton that is often plain. This version has a white printed design to add texture. Muslin can be hung behind curtains in daytime to provide privacy.

Cotton check

This is a simple but sturdy cotton fabric, suitable for all kinds of window dressings. It may be lined and interlined, but, since it is the same front and back, it can also be used for unlined items.

Hessian

This open-weave, rough-textured fabric is made of fiber from the jute plant. It is generally plain, but this example has a colored stripe woven into it. Hessian may be lined, but also works well on its own.

Chenille damask

Chenille is made from fluffy cotton yarn – the name comes from the French for "hairy caterpillar" – which gives it its soft texture. Here it is woven in damask style, with a raised pattern and flat background.

Natural linen

This beautiful fabric is made from flax. It is strong, hard-wearing, and drapes well. Linen may be finely woven or, as here, have a more open weave. It can be dyed but looks its best in natural shades.

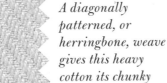

Colored and patterned fabrics

Cotton and linen mix
The combination of cotton with stronger linen fiber makes a hard-wearing, slightly stiff fabric that is particularly suitable for flat shades and edgings. The slightly raised motif adds texture.

Tapestry
Although machine-woven, this fabric possesses the ornate look of hand-woven tapestries in which each stitch is individually made. With its rich texture and pattern, it is ideal for heavy curtains or shades.

Heavy cotton weave
This thick, robust fabric is adorned with a fleur-de-lis pattern. It looks good from the front and back, making it suitable for unlined curtains and shades.

Soft blanket
The combed wool used to produce this blanket fabric makes it soft and warm. It provides good insulation at drafty windows. The same front and back, it does not need lining.

Wool damask
Like all damasks, this woolen fabric is woven to produce a raised pattern and flat background. Heavy, yet soft, it drapes well and provides good insulation. It can be used without lining.

Wool tartan
This woolen cloth is woven in plaids of different scale and patterns, each specific to a Scottish clan. Originally a clothing fabric, it is now often used for furnishings. It is warm, drapes well, and may be used without lining.

Wool check
The twill, or diagonal weave, of this woolen cloth is produced by passing the weft threads alternatively over one, then two warp threads. This smart-looking cloth is suitable for all kinds of window dressings.

Paisley
The paisley pattern is printed in many colors on a fine Egyptian cotton. Paisley originated in India but was imported into the Scottish town of Paisley. It features swirling cone or pear shapes.

Cotton chintz

Chintz is a cotton fabric that generally features a multi-colored floral print on a cream or light ground. Chintz with a glazed surface requires careful laundering.

Printed linen

Frequently used in its natural color, linen can also have patterns printed on it. This example has a dynamic foliage pattern, screen-printed in at least eight colors. It is suitable for all kinds of window dressings.

Printed cotton

The background of this cotton was overprinted to resemble a color wash overlaid with gold. Although printed, the fabric looks similar to rich velvet from a distance, showing the versatility of cotton.

Silk taffeta

A brittle, finely woven fabric, taffeta has a crisp finish. The warp and weft threads of different colors give it an everchanging surface. It drapes well and is suitable for full-length curtains.

Silk damask

Silk is the traditional material for damask, which has a special weave that produces a raised pattern and flat background. Although fine, this beautiful and elegant fabric has body and drapes well.

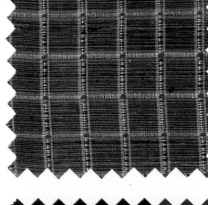

Checked silk

Silk is made from the soft, lustrous fiber made by silk worms for their cocoons. This checked silk has different-colored warp and weft threads, with other threads inlaid to create the grid effect.

Striped velvet

Velvet has a pile that generally absorbs as well as reflects light. The luxurious red stripe on this cotton example catches the light and shimmers against the mat gold of the background.

Printed velvet

Velvet always has a luxurious appearance. This example has a contemporary look and would work well as a full-length lined curtain.

The Basic Techniques

MEASURING WINDOWS

FOR SUCCESSFUL WINDOW TREATMENTS, it is vital that you take careful measurements or all the hard work in making your curtain or shade will be wasted. Always use a steel tape measure – cloth measures do not give accurate enough measurements – and make clear, concise notes of measurements (it is worth making a habit of jotting down the width first so that you do not get measurements confused).

The first stage of measuring is to decide where the support should be if it is not already in place. There are three basic choices: You can hang curtains or shades on a support attached to the wall above the frame and extending to each side, to a support attached to the window frame, or to a support within the window recess. If the support is attached to the wall or the window frame, then you must also decide whether you want your window treatment to stop at the level of the window sill or extend down to the floor.

Next you will need to determine the finished width and drop of your curtain or shade. These are the measurements you will use to work out the actual, or cut, width and drop of fabric needed, by adding amounts for seams, headings, and hems to the finished width and drop (see the tables on pp. 40–41). If using a patterned fabric, you must also allow extra fabric for matching the pattern across the fabric widths (see p. 41).

GLOSSARY OF MEASURING TERMS

Finished width: *the width of the area the curtain or shade is to cover. The curtain or shade should make this width once it is pleated or gathered.*

Finished drop: *the length of the curtain or shade once it is completed and hung.*

Cut width: *the finished width plus allowances for seams and fullness for the heading.*

Cut drop: *the finished drop plus allowances for hems and headings.*

Width of fabric: *the width of the fabric as purchased. Generally, the width of fabric you are using will be less than the cut width of your curtain or shade and so you will need to buy more than one width and join them together.*

Support: *a device such as a pole, track, or lath from which a curtain or shade hangs. It can be attached outside, on, or within the frame.*

Recessed window: *a window that is set back into the wall, so that you can hang a curtain or shade inside the recess instead of on the wall.*

Selvage: *the tightly woven edges of a width of fabric.*

Measuring for a curtain or shade that hangs from a support on the wall

A support fitted to the wall is usually positioned 4–12 in (10–30 cm) above the window and extends up to 8 in (20 cm) each side, as space permits. Measure the width of the window (A) and add the amount the support extends to each side (A1 and A2) to get the finished width. Measure the drop of the window (B) and add the distance between the support and the top of the window (B1) to get the finished drop. If you are extending your curtains to the floor, also add the distance from the sill to the floor (B2) to get the finished drop.

Deduct 1 in (2.5 cm) from finished drop if curtain is to fall just short of floor. If curtain is to drape on floor, add 6 in (15 cm).

Measuring for a curtain or shade that hangs from a support attached to the window frame

For a curtain or shade whose support is fitted to the frame, measure from one side of the frame to the other (C) to get the finished width, and from top of the frame to the sill (D) to get the finished drop. For floor-length curtains, measure from top of the frame to the floor (D plus D1) to get finished drop.

Measuring for a curtain or shade that hangs inside the window recess

For a curtain or shade whose support is fitted within the window recess, measure the distance from one side of the recess to the other (E) to get the finished width, and the distance from the top of the recess to the sill (F) to get the finished drop.

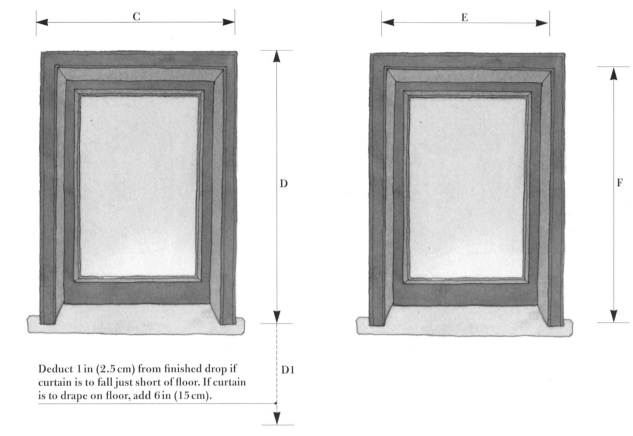

Deduct 1 in (2.5 cm) from finished drop if curtain is to fall just short of floor. If curtain is to drape on floor, add 6 in (15 cm).

Estimating fabric

Use the finished width and finished drop measurements you have made to work out the cut width and cut drop of your curtain or shade and then use them to estimate how much fabric you need to buy. Remember that if you are using a patterned fabric, you need to allow extra for matching the pattern across the widths (see p. 41).

1 *To work out cut width for curtains, multiply finished width by amount of fullness your heading requires (see p. 40) and add amounts for side hems. For shades, add amounts for seams, returns, and other extras, such as pleats (see p. 41), to finished width.*

For example:
Finished width (52 in/132 cm): A, C, or E on diagrams opposite and above
x ***allowance for heading*** *(2.5)*
= *130 in/330 cm*
+ ***allowance for side hems*** *(4 in/10 cm)*
= ***cut width*** *(134 in/340 cm)*

2 *To work out cut drop for curtains, add amounts needed for top and base hems (see p. 40) to finished drop. For shades, add amounts for base hem and for attaching top of shade to its support (see p. 41) to finished drop.*

For example:
Finished drop (74 in/188 cm): B (+B1), D + (D1), or F on diagrams opposite and above
+ ***allowance for top and base hems*** *(10 in/25 cm)*
= ***cut drop*** *(84 in/213 cm)*

3 *To calculate amount of fabric to buy, work out how many widths of fabric you need to make the required cut width. To do this, divide cut width by width of fabric you are using. Round up answer to nearest full number and multiply it by the cut drop to give the amount of yards (meters) of fabric to buy.*

For example:
Cut width (134 in/340 cm)
÷ ***width of fabric*** *(48 in/122 cm)*
= ***widths of fabric needed*** *(2.8 = 3)*
Cut drop (84 in/213 cm) x 3
= ***amount needed*** *(252 in/639 cm). For safety, buy 7 ½ yards (7 meters)*

Estimating fabric for curtains

This table tells you how much extra fabric you need to allow for different curtain styles. Once you have measured the finished width and finished drop of your curtain (see pp. 38–39), you can then work out the cut width and cut drop of your curtain by adding on the extra, depending on the style of curtain you are making. Remember that most curtains require more than one width of fabric, so you also need to allow extra for joining fabric widths (see p. 43).

Heading type	Cut width See individual projects for details on side hems.	Cut drop For each curtain	Notes
Slot heading	1½ to 2 times the finished width	The finished drop + 4¾ in (12 cm) for hem allowances + 1½–2 in (3–5 cm) for sleeve at top of curtain	This accommodates a slim pole of about ¾ in (2 cm) in diameter. Generally add about twice the circumference of the pole to the drop to allow for the slot.
Gathered heading 1-in (2.5-cm) tape	2½ times the finished width	The finished drop + 8 in (20 cm) for base hem + 2 in (5 cm) for top hem	There is only one row of pockets for the curtain hooks.
Pencil-pleat heading 3-in (7.5-cm) tape	2½ times the finished width	The finished drop + 8 in (20 cm) for base hem + 3 in (7.5 cm) for top hem	Hooks can be inserted into any one of three rows of pockets.
Hand-sewn hooks	1½ to 2 times the finished width	The finished drop + 8 in (20 cm) for base hem + 2 in (5 cm) for top hem	If a "panel" effect is required, curtains headed with hand-sewn hooks need be little more than the width of the window.
Eyelets	1½ to 2 times the finished width	The finished drop + 8 in (20 cm) for base hem + 2 in (5 cm) for top hem	As a rule, eyelets should be set 4–6 in (10–15 cm) apart.
French or Goblet pleats	2½ times the finished width	The finished drop + 8 in (20 cm) for base hem + 7–8 in (18–20 cm) for top hem	This allows for about four or five pleats per fabric width.
Box pleats	3 times the finished width, if the whole width is to be box pleated 2–2½ times the finished width, if the pleats are to be spaced out	The finished drop + 8 in (20 cm) for base hem + 7–8 in (18–20 cm) for top hem	The width of the fabric must be divisible by the width of the front of one box pleat. For example, if a pleat measures 4 in (10 cm) across the front, the fabric has to be divided into equal 4-in (10-cm) spaces.

Estimating fabric for shades

This table is a guide to estimating fabric amounts for the main types of shade. Many flat shades can be made within one standard fabric width, but wide or pleated shades will need more. The measurements provided below are general guides. For specific instructions look at the instructions given for the shade projects.

Shade type	Cut width	Cut drop	Notes
Shade with lath top	Finished width + 4 in (10 cm) for side hems	Finished drop + 2 in (5 cm) for base hem + 10 in (25 cm) for attaching top of shade to the lath. If the shade has returns (see p. 56), allow 2 in (5 cm) for attaching fabric to lath.	Allow additional lining fabric for rod pockets. Each pocket measures 4¾ in (12 cm) long by the width of the shade.
Slot-head shade	Finished width + 4 in (10 cm) for side hems	Finished drop + 2 in (5 cm) for base hem + 3–10 in (7.5–25 cm) for sleeve at top, depending on size of pole.	Make sure you allow enough in the drop to make a comfortable sleeve for the pole.
Pleated shade	Finished width + 4 in (10 cm) for side hems + 4 in (10 cm) for returns + amount for each pleat, for example, 8 in (20 cm)	Finished drop + 2 in (5 cm) for base hem + 10 in (25 cm) for attaching the top of shade to the lath. If the shade has returns, see above.	Pleated shades often look best with some fullness at the base, so allow another 8 in (20 cm) on the drop.
Inverted-pleat shade	Finished width + 8–12 in (20–30 cm) for central inverted pleat + 4 in (10 cm) for side hems + 1½ in (4 cm) for seams to join sides to central pleat	Finished drop + 2 in (5 cm) for base hem + 10 in (25 cm) for attaching the top of the shade to a lath. If the shade has returns, see above.	

Allowing for repeat patterns

The design on patterned fabric must line up exactly across joined widths. Take this into account when calculating fabric quantities – you need extra fabric because some is discarded in order to match the pattern.

Once you have calculated the cut drop (see pp. 38–39), measure the length of a complete pattern – this may be noted on the label with fabric. Divide the cut drop by the pattern length. Round up this number to the next full number and multiply by the pattern length to obtain the length that needs to be cut.

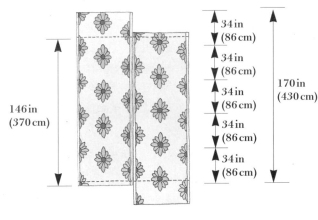

For example, if you have a cut drop of 146 in (370 cm) and a pattern length of 34 in (86 cm), divide 146 (370) by 34 (86) to get 4.3. Round this up to 5. Multiply the pattern length of 34 (86) by 5. This means that you will need to cut a length of 170 in (430 cm), so that you have enough to match up the pattern across widths.

PREPARING FABRIC

Cutting fabric

Fabrics are usually supplied rolled around a cardboard tube, making them easier to handle when laying them out for cutting. Before cutting, check the fabric for any faults and double-check all measurements. Take great care when cutting – accuracy at this stage means fewer problems later on. Use sharp scissors, preferably with long blades, such as those used by professional curtain makers or dressmakers. A good-quality pair will last for years.

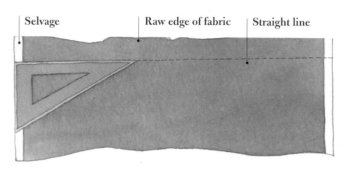

Selvage   Raw edge of fabric   Straight line

1 *Straighten raw edge of fabric by using a T-square or any other right-angled object to make a straight line that is square to the selvage.*

2 *To divide fabric into the cut drops required, first measure and mark the distance of the cut drop down the selvage and down the center of the fabric width. Make a line across the fabric by joining the marks with pencil or chalk, using a long rule. Repeat until you have marked all the cut drops needed and cut along the lines with sharp scissors.*

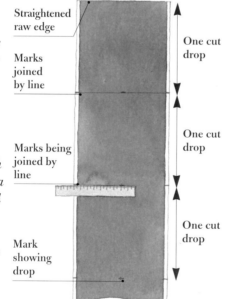

Straightened raw edge

Marks joined by line

Marks being joined by line

Mark showing drop

One cut drop

One cut drop

One cut drop

CUTTING SHEER FABRICS

When cutting sheer or loosely woven fabrics, draw out a thread across the width as a guide to help you cut straight. Cut along the path of this thread.

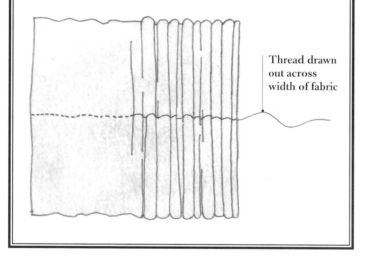

Thread drawn out across width of fabric

Combining widths and half widths

Once you have cut out your fabric, combine widths as necessary. If a pair of curtains requires three widths, cut one fabric width in half and make each curtain of one and a half widths (below left). If a shade needs more than one width, make the shade with one full width at the center and a part width at each side (below).

Widths for curtains
If using part widths and full widths of fabric, always place the part width at the outside of the curtain and the full width at the center.

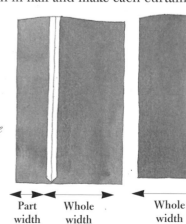

Part width   Whole width   Whole width   Part width

Widths for shades
Avoid using narrow strips to make up the width of a shade. Cut down center panel so that smaller sections are at least quarter fabric widths.

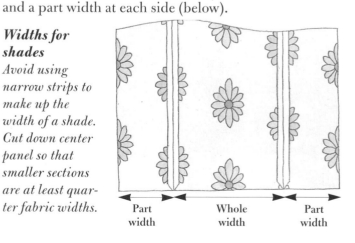

Part width   Whole width   Part width

Joining fabric widths

You can join together fabric widths for lined and interlined curtains or shades by simply machine-stitching the two widths together. For unlined curtains or shades, use French seams (see p. 47) for joining widths so that the raw edges are neatly concealed.

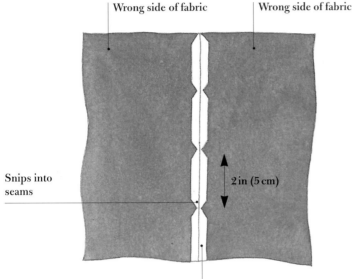

Wrong side of fabric

Wrong side of fabric

Snips into seams

2 in (5 cm)

Seams pressed flat

Place widths right sides together, leaving a seam allowance of 1 in (2.5 cm). Machine-stitch parallel to the selvage, or raw edge. Press seams flat. If fabric puckers when stitched or if selvage appears tight, it may affect the way the fabric hangs. Snip into the seams at 2-in (5-cm) intervals to allow some give, but be careful not to cut into the stitching.

Weighting a curtain

Curtains, especially floor-length ones, hang best if they are weighted down with curtain weights that are stitched into the base hem. The weights help the curtain keep its shape, especially when it has a full heading.

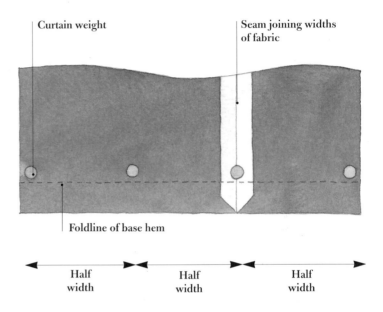

Curtain weight

Seam joining widths of fabric

Foldline of base hem

Half width

Half width

Half width

Insert weights at each corner of the curtain and at half-width intervals across its base. You should cover the weights in lining fabric and then stitch them into the base hem by hand (see p. 46).

Interlining and lining

Allow for the same amount of interlining and lining as the main fabric when estimating how much to buy – even though you use slightly less. If possible, buy lining in the same width as the main fabric so that seams match. Interlining seams are concealed by the lining, so its width matters less.

Interlining
Join interlining widths with a lapped seam (see p. 47). Before starting to make the curtain, attach interlining to the main fabric, using locking in stitch (see p. 44). Lock in the interlining at seams joining widths of fabric and halfway between fabric widths.

Lining
Cut and join lining widths as for fabric. Press seams flat. If possible, match joins of the lining with those of the fabric. On large curtains or wide shades lock in lining as interlining.

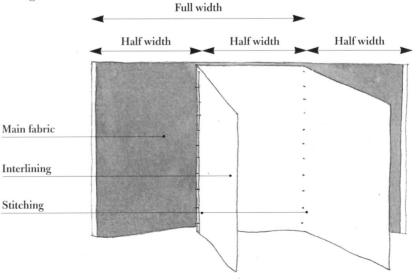

Full width

Half width

Half width

Half width

Main fabric

Interlining

Stitching

HAND STITCHES

Basting stitch

This is a temporary stitch used to hold together several layers of fabric as a more secure alternative to pinning.

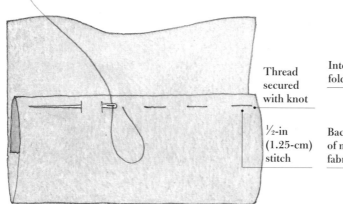

Thread secured with knot

½-in (1.25-cm) stitch

Secure thread with a knot inside hem and make a series of straight stitches, each about ½ in (1.25 cm) long. To remove the stitching, cut off the knot and pull out the thread.

Locking-in stitch

Use this stitch to secure lining or interlining loosely to the back of wide curtains or shades to prevent the separate layers ballooning apart when they are hanging.

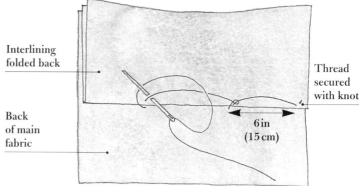

Interlining folded back

Back of main fabric

Thread secured with knot

6 in (15 cm)

Secure thread at back of interlining. Put needle through fold of lining close to edge and take up a few threads of the main fabric. Put needle through the loop of thread, leaving some slack thread, and make the next stitch about 6 in (15 cm) farther down.

Herringbone stitch

This neat stitch keeps hems that are to be covered by lining flat and in place. For right-handed people, stitches are worked from left to right with the needle pointing left.

Thread secured inside hem

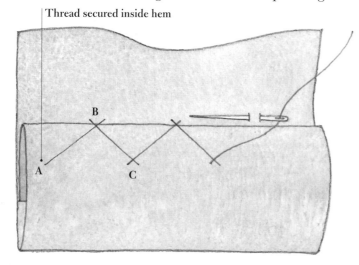

B

A

C

Working from left to right with the needle pointing left, secure thread inside hem and bring needle through hem edge (A). Make a small stitch in the fabric directly above hem edge and about 1 in (2.5 cm) to the right (B), with needle pointing left. Take the next stitch 1 in (2.5 cm) to the right in hem edge (C), again with needle pointing left. Repeat sequence of alternating stitches as shown until you reach end of hem.

Slipstitch

Use this stitch to sew a hem in place invisibly. Here, the size of the stitch is exaggerated so you can see how it works; in reality you should hardly be able to see it.

Thread secured inside hem

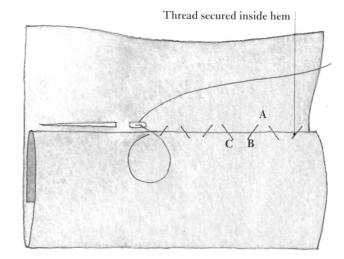

A

C B

Working from right to left, secure thread inside hem and bring needle out near folded edge. Insert needle into main fabric and make a small stitch (A). Catch only a few threads at a time so the stitching does not show on the right side. Insert needle back into fold about ⅛ in (3 mm) from first stitch (B). Pass needle through fold and bring out again about ½ in (1.25 cm) from first pair of stitches (C). Repeat the sequence.

Chain stitch

This stitch consists of a small chain of threads that you can use to provide a loose link between lining and fabric at the base hem of a curtain to prevent them from billowing apart.

Thread secured inside hem

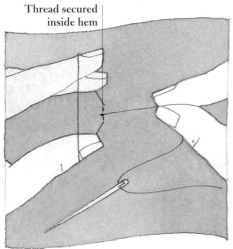 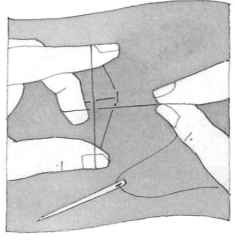 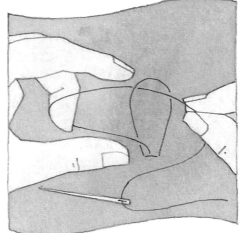

1 *Secure thread in hem with a couple of small stitches. Take a third stitch but do not pull it through. Leave the loop loose. Hold the loop around the first finger and thumb of your left hand (or right, if you are left-handed). Hold the needle, with thread attached, in your other hand.*

2 *Use the second finger of your left hand to pull the lower part of the thread held by your right hand through the loop.*

3 *Release your finger and thumb so that the loop tightens around thread as you pull on the thread with your right hand. Repeat to form a continuous chain of about 2 in (5 cm). When chain is right length, take needle through loop and pull tight to secure chain. Stitch end of chain to underside of lining hem.*

Stabbing stitch

Use this stitch to hold several layers of fabric together – for example, at the base of a goblet pleat (see p. 51).

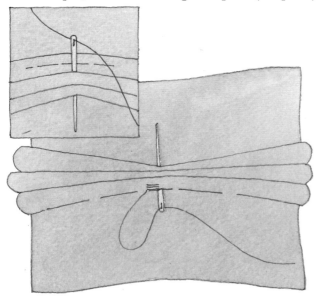

Knot end of thread and pass needle in between the layers so that the knot lies at the center of the pleat (see inset). Pass the needle back and forth on the same spot through all the layers, until you have a neat, firm stitch holding all the layers in place.

Couching stitch

Use this stitch to attach rings or hooks to fabric. Use a double thread for extra strength.

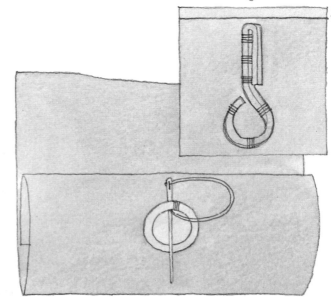

Using double thread, secure the thread in the fabric and make a simple stitch over and over in the same place until the ring is firmly attached. To attach a hook, make several groups of stitches all around the hook and pass the needle from one group of stitches to the next without breaking the thread (see inset).

HEMS AND SEAMS

Double curtain hem with interlining

Use this hem when adding interlining to a curtain. The double hem locks the interlining securely and neatly to the curtain before the lining is stitched on top. Add in curtain weights at this stage if they are needed.

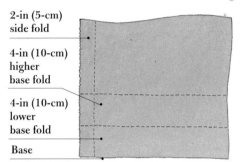

2-in (5-cm) side fold

4-in (10-cm) higher base fold

4-in (10-cm) lower base fold

Base

1 *Lay fabric right side down. At the base, fold up 4 in (10 cm) and press. Fold up by 4 in (10 cm) again and press. Press in 2 in (5 cm) at the sides. Open out the folds as above.*

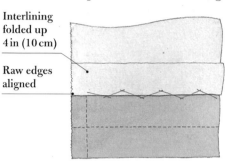

Interlining folded up 4 in (10 cm)

Raw edges aligned

2 *Lay interlining on fabric, aligning edges of interlining with raw edge at sides and lower foldline along base of fabric. Fold interlining up 4 in (10 cm) and secure interlining to fabric along fold with herringbone stitch (see p. 44).*

Interlining folded in 2 in (5 cm)

Raw edge of interlining

3 *Fold interlining down again and press it in 2 in (5 cm) at the side. Herringbone-stitch raw edge in place along lower foldline at base of fabric and along folded edge at foldline running up side of fabric.*

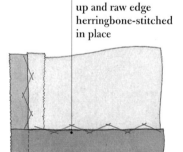

Base of fabric turned up and raw edge herringbone-stitched in place

4 *At base of curtain, turn fabric up at first foldline and press. Herringbone-stitch raw edge of fabric in place.*

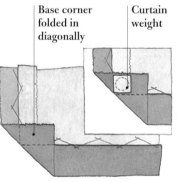

Base corner folded in diagonally

Curtain weight

5 *Fold base corner in diagonally, aligning fold-line at side of fabric with raw edge of base. Stitch in curtain weight if needed (see inset).*

Side hem folded in and herringbone-stitched

6 *Fold in side hem of curtain again, along 2-in (5-cm) foldline. Press and herringbone-stitch it in place.*

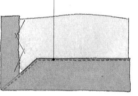

Base hem folded up and slipstitched

7 *Turn in second fold of base hem and press. Stitch across the mitered corner and secure base hem with slipstitch (see p. 44). Repeat Steps 5–7 to miter corner at other side of fabric in the same way.*

Double lining hem

A double hem gives a firmer base to a lining and is useful in case the lining shrinks and needs to be let down.

Fold up 2 in (5 cm) at base of lining and press flat. Fold up base again to make a double 2-in (5-cm) hem. Press and machine-stitch along top, close to fold.

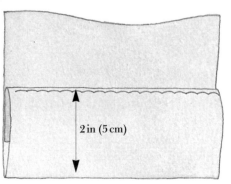

2 in (5 cm)

Covering curtain weights

Curtains hang best if they have weights along their base in the corners and at half-width intervals (see p. 43).

To cover a weight, place it on a piece of lining (near right). Fold lining over the weight and stitch around all four sides (far right). You can then hand-stitch them into the corner hems (see Step 5 above).

Making a French seam

This seam is useful for joining widths for an unlined curtain or shade. It hides the raw edges of the fabric.

Place pieces to be joined wrong sides together, matching any pattern, and baste together (see p. 44). Machine-stitch ¼ in (6 mm) from raw edges (above left). Turn the fabric so that right sides are facing. Press and stitch ⅜ in (1 cm) away from folded edge, so that the raw edges are concealed inside the seam, making a neat finish (above right). Open the fabric out and press the seam flat on the wrong side. Remove basting stitches.

Making a lapped seam

Use this seam to join bulky fabrics, such as interlining, where the stitchline will not be visible.

Place both pieces of fabric to be joined right side up so that one overlaps the other by about ¾ in (2 cm). Machine-stitch the two pieces together, using either a zigzag or a straight stitch.

Making piping

Use piping to make a neat, practical finish along the side, top, and bottom edges of both curtains and shades. Cut your fabric on the bias so that it has the flexibility to stretch around curves and corners.

1 *To cut bias strips, first fold the fabric on the diagonal to mark the cross-grain (bias) of the fabric. Press the fold.*

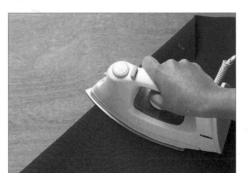

2 *Open fold and, with foldline as guide, use pins to mark parallel lines 2 in (5 cm) apart, diagonally across fabric. Cut along lines to create 2-in (5-cm) wide strips.*

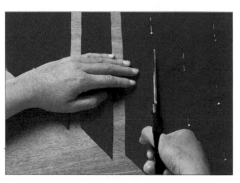

3 *Pin two strips right sides together as shown. The strips should be at right angles so that the straight grain matches at the short edges.*

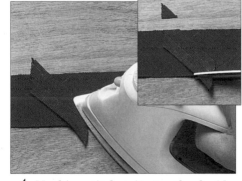

4 *Machine-stitch strips together beside the pins and press seam open. Trim off excess corners of fabric (see inset). Continue joining strips in this way to make the required length.*

5 *Fold strip in half lengthwise, wrong sides together. Place regular piping cord into the folded fabric. Using a piping or half foot, machine-stitch edges of strip, keeping close to the cord.*

HEADINGS

Making a slot heading

For this heading, make a "sleeve" of fabric into which a slim pole slides. The slot can be at the top or an inch or two (2–5 cm) below (see Step 2).

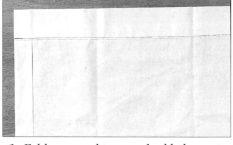

1 *Fold over and press a double hem at the top of curtain or shade. Allow for the slot to be at least ½ in (1.25 cm) bigger than the circumference of pole. Machine-stitch the base of hem and insert the pole.*

2 *For a slot lower down, fold over a double hem 1 in (2.5 cm) deeper than in Step 1, and make two parallel lines of stitching, one 1 in (2.5 cm) from the top and the second at the base of the hem.*

Making a pencil-pleat heading

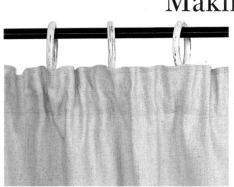

This heading is made with 3-in (7.5-cm) tape, which gathers the curtain into pleats.

1 *Turn over a single hem at the top of the curtain. The hem should be less than 3 in (7.5 cm) so the raw edge is covered by tape. Align the tape with the top of curtain, tucking it under at each end but leaving the strings free. Knot strings at one end and secure them beneath the tape with several lines of machine stitching. Leave the strings at the other end free. Machine-stitch along the top and bottom edges of the tape to attach it to the curtain.*

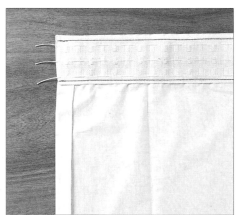

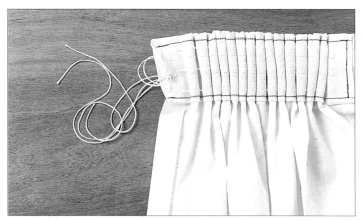

2 *Pull up loose strings of tape until the curtain is the required width. Make sure that pleats are evenly distributed across the width. Knot strings, but do not finally secure until you have checked the width of the curtain.*

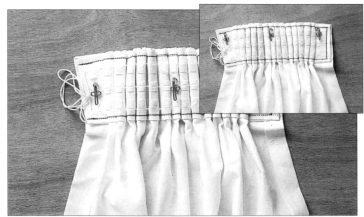

3 *Place hooks in pockets, one at each end of the curtain and the rest about 3 in (7.5 cm) apart. The hooks are generally placed in the middle row of pockets on the tape. Alternatively, they can be placed in the top (see inset) or lower row, depending on whether you want to hide the support.*

Making a gathered heading

This simple heading is made with 1-in (2.5-cm) tape, which is stitched to the back of the curtain.

Position the tape at least 1 in (2.5 cm) down from the top of curtain, the exact distance depending on the situation. Here, the top edge of the tape is set 2 in (5 cm) down. Follow the instructions for the pencil-pleat heading (see Steps 1–3, p. 48) to attach the heading and prepare the curtain for hanging. With 1-in (2.5-cm) tape there is no choice in where you place the hooks since there is only one row of pockets.

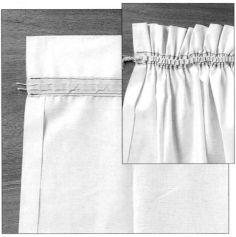

Hand-sewing hooks

No tape is used on this heading. Instead, long hooks, usually brass, are hand-sewn directly to the back of the curtain.

Position hooks at the top of curtain, leaving about 6–8 in (15–20 cm) between each hook. The top of the hook should not project above top of curtain, unless hooks are intended to be seen (see left).

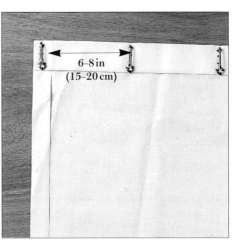

Making an eyelet heading

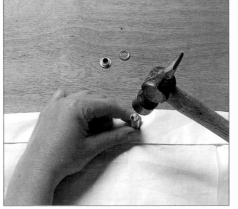

This heading is made with a punch and dye set. It punches a hole in the fabric and fits the two parts of the brass eyelet, one on each side of the fabric. Position them ½ in (1.25 cm) from curtain top at intervals of 3–5 in (7.5–12.5 cm).

1 *With the fabric right side down, place the punch underneath it at the position you want the eyelet. With its rounded side down, position the dye on top of it on the other side of the fabric and tap firmly with a hammer to make the hole.*

2 *Place the center part of the eyelet under the fabric so that it projects through the hole from the right side (see inset). Place the ring over it and position the dye into it, pointed side down. Tap firmly with the hammer to fit into place and complete the eyelet.*

Making French pleats

This smart-looking heading is made up of groups of three pleats and is most suitable for long curtains. Fusible buckram – stiffened fabric that can be sealed to fabric by the heat of an iron – is used to give shape to the pleated heading.

1 *Fold the top of the curtain over to the wrong side at the finished dropline and press. Here, about 7 in (18 cm) of fabric is folded over.*

2 *Open out the fold. Take some fusible buckram about 4 in (10 cm) wide and 6 in (15 cm) longer than the width of the curtain. Place the fusible buckram across the top of the curtain so that its bottom edge aligns with the finished dropline.*

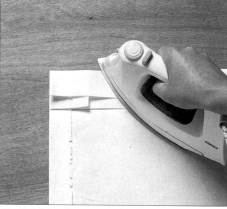

3 *Fold in the excess fusible buckram at each end. Fold the excess fabric at the top over the fusible buckram and press. The heat of the iron seals the fusible buckram to the fabric.*

4 *Fold over the covered fusible buckram so that the finished dropline is at the top of the curtain and press again.*

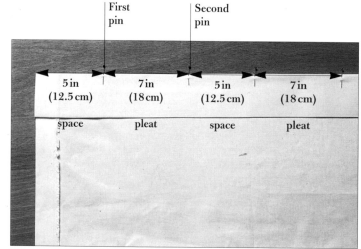

First pin | Second pin
5 in (12.5 cm) | 7 in (18 cm) | 5 in (12.5 cm) | 7 in (18 cm)
space | pleat | space | pleat

5 *Mark positions of pleats with pins. The distance between the edge of the curtain and the start of the first pleat should be the same as the space between each pleat. This should generally be 4–6 in (10–15 cm) but can be adjusted to suit your curtain. Here, the space between each pleat is 5 in (12.5 cm) and amount allowed for each pleat is 7 in (18 cm).*

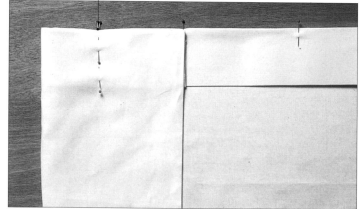

First and second pins together

6 *Fold the heading with wrong sides together so that the first pin meets the second pin. Pin in place. Take the third pin to the fourth pin and continue to fold and pin the remaining pleats in the same way. Machine-stitch each pleat from the top of the curtain to the base of fusible buckram section.*

7 *Turn curtain over so right side is uppermost. Flatten pleat and pinch the middle into a pleat (see inset). Bring up material at each side to make three pleats of equal size.*

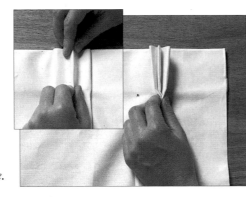

8 *Secure folds together at base of pleat with stabbing stitch (see p. 45). At top of pleat, stitch each of the three folds in place. Repeat Steps 7–8 to make the remaining pleats.*

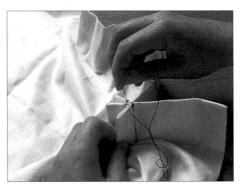

Making goblet pleats

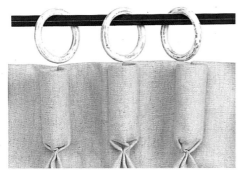

This elegant heading consists of round pleats that are spaced out along the top of the curtain. They are stuffed to keep their shape.

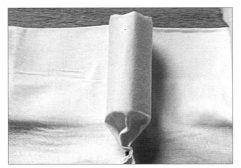

1 *Follow Steps 1–6 for French pleats (see p. 50) and, with fabric right side up, pinch base of pleat together and secure with stabbing stitch (see p. 45).*

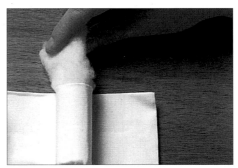

2 *Leave top of pleat open and stuff it with a roll of batting. Push batting well down into the pleat to give it shape. Repeat with rest of pleats.*

Making box pleats

These hand-sewn pleats give an attractive neat finish, but are not suitable for heavy fabrics.

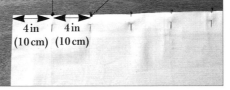

First pin   Second pin

4 in (10 cm)   4 in (10 cm)

1 *Divide width of curtain into equal spaces, marked with pins on the front. The example here shows pins 4 in (10 cm) apart, to make box pleats measuring 4 in (10 cm) across the front.*

First and second pins together

2 *With the front of the curtain facing you, take the first pin to meet the second pin.*

Third pin

3 *Then take the third pin to meet the second pin and pin them in place to make a pleat.*

Fourth and fifth pins

4 *Take fourth pin to meet fifth pin and sixth pin to meet fifth pin to make a second pleat. Repeat the process until you have pinned all the pleats.*

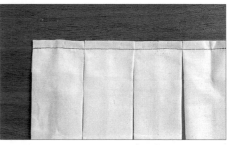

5 *Press pleats across top of curtain and machine-stitch across all the pleats, about 1 in (2.5 cm) down from the top of the curtain, to keep them in place.*

HANGING TECHNIQUES
Putting up a pole

Poles are supported on wooden or metal brackets that are fitted to the wall above the window or to the window frame itself. If there is space, the pole should extend to each side so that the curtain can be pulled back off the window. Curtain rings are threaded onto the pole, with one at each end beyond the bracket to hold the curtains in place. For single curtains, place a ring outside the bracket at one end only, so the curtain can be pulled right back. Poles are available in many different styles and thicknesses and can be cut to the width required for your window. The instructions here give a general guide to putting up poles that you can adapt to your particular situation. Most poles also come with manufacturer's instructions that explain exactly how to fix the brackets and pole.

1 *Mark the position of the pole above the window. This distance should be about 4–6 in (10–15 cm), but will vary according to the situation.*

2 *Mark the position of the brackets to each side of the window, making sure they are aligned. These should be placed about 4 in (10 cm) from the molding.*

3 *Fix one bracket to the wall following manufacturer's instructions. Wooden ones have a metal wallplate that is fixed to the wall first (see inset), and then the bracket is screwed onto the wallplate.*

4 *Check the pole in position on one bracket, ensuring it is straight. Fix other bracket. Tighten screws on underside of brackets into the pole to keep it firmly in place. Leave end rings off the pole.*

5 *Put one curtain ring on each end of pole beyond bracket. Fit finials to each end of pole so that ring is between the bracket and finial. Then you are ready to hang the curtains.*

Pole with architrave bracket
As well as being suitable for use on a wall, architrave, or molding, brackets are thin enough to fit on the frame of a window. You need them when there is no room to fit brackets above or to the sides of a window, or when the wall is too crumbly to support the weight of curtains. They are usually made of brass or other metal and are fitted to the frame with matching screws. Simply position the bracket, mark the screw holes, drill the holes, and attach the bracket with screws. The front of the bracket screws into the pole to keep it in place.

Putting up a pole in a window recess

There are special brackets, known as "thimble" brackets, for fitting a slim pole in a window recess. These encase each end of the pole and are completely hidden by, for example, a slot-head curtain. There are also brackets for attaching the ends of poles to a side wall when there is no room to attach it to the wall the window is in (see Step 3).

1 *Mark the position of the brackets on the sides of the recess – the distance down depends on the amount of fabric above the slot. Fit the brackets with the screws provided.*

2 *Measure the distance between the two brackets and cut the pole to about ⅛ in (3 mm) less than this distance. Fit the pole into the brackets and screw in the sleeve part of the bracket to hold the pole in place.*

3 *The result is an extremely neat fitting that can be used for a light-weight curtain with small rings or a slot heading. For a larger pole fixed to an adjacent wall at one end, use a recess holder bracket (see inset).*

USING A TRACK

There are many types of tracks available that can be fitted either to the wall above the window or along the top of the window frame. The simplest type (see below) has small wall brackets that are screwed into the wall at regular intervals and then the track, which has gliders for hooks, simply clips into the bracket. If you put up a track yourself, make sure you follow the manufacturer's instructions carefully. If you need to bend a track around a curved or bay window, or to conceal it behind a fascia, it is advisable to get it fitted by a professional.

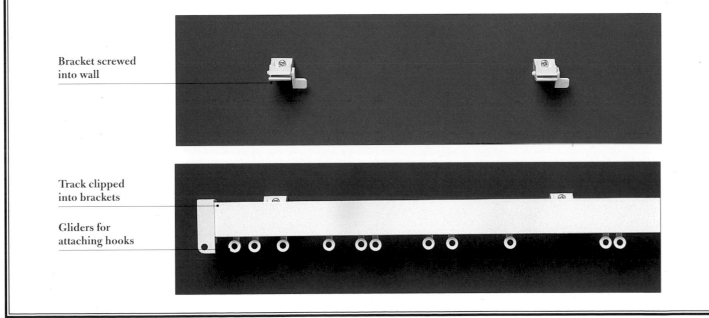

Bracket screwed into wall

Track clipped into brackets

Gliders for attaching hooks

Cording a shade

The basic principles of cording a shade are the same whatever the type. Two or three lengths of cord are knotted to rings attached at or near the base of the shade and run up the back through a series of rings and eventually a screw eye attached to the lath at the top of the shade. The cords then all go across the top to one side of the shade, where the loose ends are threaded through a brass drop weight. To raise the shade, pull the drop weight downward and wind the excess cord around a cleat attached to the wall to keep the shade in a raised position.

Roman shade (see pp. 96–99)

This shade has dowel rods that run across the back of the shade at regular intervals. They sit in pockets (see p. 98) that are stitched to the lining.

1 Position the lowest rod pocket 4 in (10 cm) above the base of the shade and space them at intervals of 8–12 in (20–30 cm), with the highest one at least 14 in (35 cm) from the top.

2 Hand-stitch rings to the pockets up the center of shade and a row 2 in (5 cm) from both edges.

3 Attach the screw eyes to the lath (see p. 55), directly in line with the rows of rings. Attach another screw eye 1 in (2.5 cm) in from the edge of the lath on the side where the strings will be.

4 Use one piece of cord for each row of rings. Attach each cord to bottom ring and thread it through rings above, through screw eye at top, and through adjacent screw eyes to reach the additional screw eye at the end of the lath.

5 With cords taut, pass them into drop weight. Trim off any excess and secure with a knot.

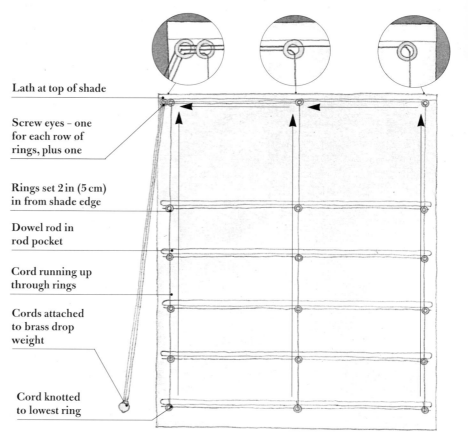

Lath at top of shade

Screw eyes – one for each row of rings, plus one

Rings set 2 in (5 cm) in from shade edge

Dowel rod in rod pocket

Cord running up through rings

Cords attached to brass drop weight

Cord knotted to lowest ring

Panel shade (see pp. 108–11)

This shade has no dowel rods and only two rows of rings.

• Position each row of rings 4 in (10 cm) from sides and space them at intervals of about 6 in (15 cm), with the lowest one 2 in (5 cm) from the base and highest one at least 8 in (20 cm) from the top.

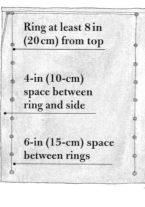

Ring at least 8 in (20 cm) from top

4-in (10-cm) space between ring and side

6-in (15-cm) space between rings

Panel shade with rod (see pp. 104–7)

This shade is like the panel shade (above) but has a dowel rod along the base.

• Position rod 6 in (15 cm) above base and position rings as with panel shade, except that lowest ring in each row should be 6 in (15 cm) above rod.

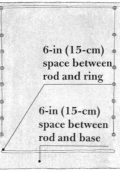

6-in (15-cm) space between rod and ring

6-in (15-cm) space between rod and base

Inverted-pleat shade (see pp. 112–17)

This shade has two rows of rings and no dowel rods.

• Position each row of rings 4 in (10 cm) from sides and space them at about 12-in (30-cm) intervals, with the lowest one 2 in (5 cm) from the base and highest one at least 18 in (45 cm) from the top.

Ring at least 18 in (45 cm) from top

4-in (10-cm) space between ring and side

12-in (30-cm) space between rings

Shade with several inverted pleats (see pp. 118–23)

This shade has extra rows of rings running up each pleat.

• Position as for inverted-pleat shade, adding extra rows of rings as required.

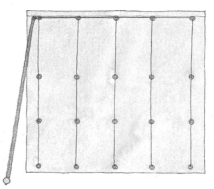

Fixing a lath to a shade

A lath for a shade is generally a piece of 2 x 1-in (5 x 2.5-cm) timber, cut to the finished width of the shade. Slimmer laths, measuring 1 x 1 in (2.5 x 2.5 cm), can be used for lightweight shades. For covering a 2 x 1-in (5 x 2.5-cm) lath, allow at least 10 in (25 cm) of fabric above the finished dropline of the shade.

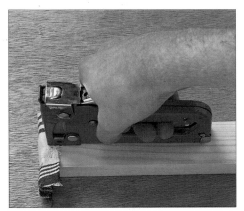

1 *Cut two pieces of the shade fabric about 3 in (7.5 cm) square. Wrap one piece around the end of the lath and, using a staple gun, fix it to the top and bottom of the wide face.*

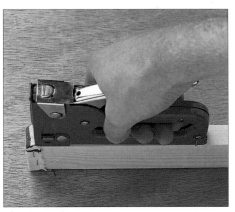

2 *On the narrow faces of the lath, fold the fabric over neatly like a parcel and staple in place. Repeat at other end. If the shade is to be ceiling-fixed, drill screw holes through the lath (see p. 56).*

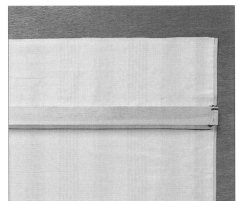

3 *Mark the finished dropline on the wrong side of the shade. Position the lath so that the bottom of it aligns with the marked dropline (top of shade).*

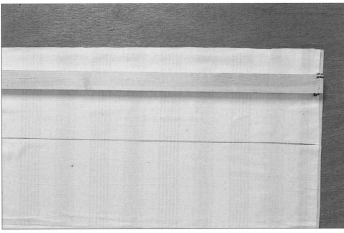

4 *Roll the lath away from the finished dropline toward the top of the shade. Roll it over once completely so that the same side as before is face up.*

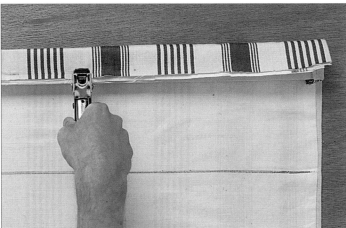

5 *Fold the fabric extending above over the lath, trimming off any excess if necessary. Staple the fabric to the lath.*

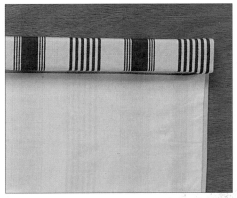

6 *Roll the lath back toward the marked dropline until it rests in the correct position, with the top of the lath at the marked dropline.*

7 *Using a bradawl (see p. 124), mark the positions of screw eyes for cording the shade. These should align with the rows of cording rings on the shade.*

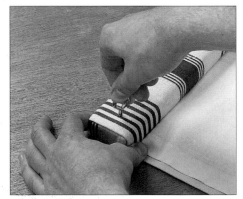

8 *Insert the screw eyes into the marked holes. Make sure that they are not too tight or they will pull on the fabric.*

Covering a lath for a shade with returns

Use this method when the rows of cording rings are close to the sides of the shade and you want to hide them with a return. The lath itself is neatly covered in lining fabric and the shade fabric extends around the ends of the lath. For this type of fixing you need to allow for an extra 2 in (5 cm) of fabric above the finished dropline.

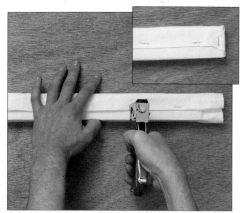

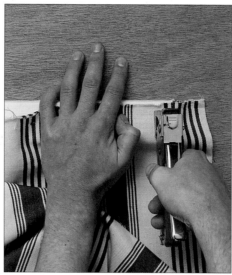

1 *To cover a standard 2 x 1-in (5 x 2.5-cm) lath, cut a piece of lining material about 7 in (18 cm) wide by the length of the lath plus about 4 in (10 cm) for turning over the ends. Wrap this around the lath, turning under the raw edges, and staple in place. Fold over the fabric at each end like a parcel and staple in place (see inset).*

2 *Position the shade, right side up, on the wide face of the covered lath, leaving about 2 in (5 cm) at each end to fold around the side of the lath. Staple the fabric to the lath.*

3 *Wrap the return at either end neatly around the end of the lath as shown and staple in place. Repeat at other end and insert screw eyes as in Steps 7–8 of "Fixing a lath to a shade" (see p. 55).*

Ceiling-fixing a lath

You can fix a shade to the ceiling simply by inserting a screw through the lath into the ceiling above. This is particularly useful when you want to hang a shade at the front of a recess, or when there is not enough room on the window frame beside the window to use angle brackets (see p. 57). Use wall plugs to make the fixing more solid.

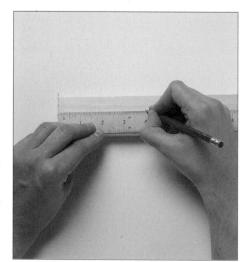

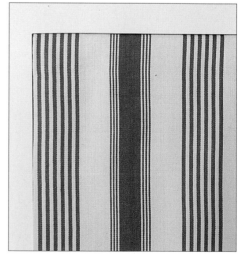

1 *Before the lath is covered, mark the positions of screw holes at least 4 in (10 cm) from each end on the wide surface of the lath. Avoid the positions for screw eyes. Drill holes through the lath.*

2 *Having covered the lath (see p. 55) and cut away the fabric to reveal the drilled holes, place the lath in position and mark the screw holes in the ceiling. Drill holes in the ceiling and, using wall plugs, insert screws through the lath and into the ceiling as shown.*

3 *Here, the finished shade hangs flush with the front of the recess, giving a neat finish. You could also use this method to attach a shade directly to the ceiling in a room.*

Face-fixing a lath on angle brackets

The completed lath, with shade, is supported on angle brackets fixed to the sides of the window or wall.
The example shown here is in a recess, but the same method applies for face-fixing a lath to a wall.

1 *Take the completed shade and lath and position it above the window. Mark the base of the lath on each side as a guide for fixing the brackets.*

2 *Position the bracket so the top aligns with the pencil mark for the base of the lath. Mark the positions of the screw holes. Repeat at the other side of the window.*

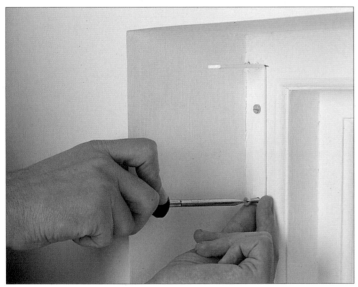

3 *Drill the holes and position the bracket so that the top aligns with the pencil mark. Insert the screws and tighten. Repeat at the other side of the recess.*

4 *Place the shade into the recess so that the lath rests on the fixed brackets. Mark the position of the screw hole in the bracket on the base of the lath. Repeat at the other side.*

5 *Take the shade off the brackets. Insert a bradawl (see p. 124) through the fabric and into the lath at the marked point. Repeat at the other end of the lath.*

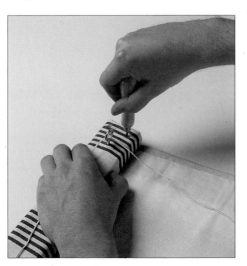

6 *Put the lath back into place on top of the brackets and insert screws through the bracket and into the lath at each end to fix the shade in place.*

The Projects

UNLINED CURTAINS

THESE ARE the simplest curtains of all – panels of fabric that hang from a slim pole stretching across the top of the window. The curtains have double hems at the sides and base, and a sleeve along the top through which the pole is slotted.

The curtains can be pushed open to the sides of the window, but a shimmery translucent fabric – such as the cream cotton muslin used here – admits enough light for them to stay permanently pulled closed if desired.

Type of window

• This style of curtain suits almost any type of window or space. It works particularly well on small windows, where you should avoid elaborate treatments, or on larger windows, where you want to keep the look simple.

• Use sheer curtains as a decorative element on their own or to hang behind a set of heavy outer curtains. If making floor-length curtains, allow plenty of excess length so that they trail on the ground – this type of curtain looks unattractive suspended above the floor.

• Unlined sheer curtains make excellent light diffusers. Use them to protect furniture or other fabrics in the room from strong sunlight, or to obscure an unappealing view.

Type of fabric

• Choose plain fabrics or a fabric that looks the same front and back, such as cotton gingham. Avoid fabrics that show the workings of a complicated weave or printed pattern on the back.

• Heavy, open-weave, textured fabrics, such as hessian, also make excellent unlined curtains.

Options

• Vary the look of these curtains by using 1-in (2.5-cm) heading tape to create a gathered effect and by hanging the curtain on a pole with rings.

• Instead of using a sheer fabric that lets the light in, try traditional checked blankets for warmth and coziness.

• Make slim borders down the leading edges to add color and contrast.

WHAT YOU WILL NEED

Fabric for each curtain

Width
*Finished width of curtain (see pp. 38–39),
plus 3 in (8 cm) for hem allowances*

Length
*Finished drop of curtain (see pp. 38–39),
plus 4¾ in (12 cm) for hem allowances, plus
allowance for slot at the top (see p. 40)*

Accessories

Pole
*Slim pole cut to fit within the window space and
attached to the sides of the recess with thimble
brackets (see p. 53)*

Making the curtains

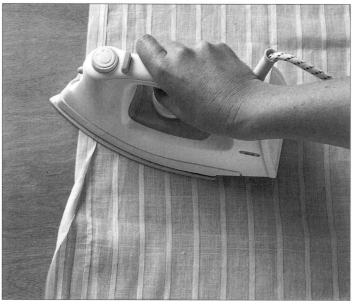

1 *When working with sheer or very light fabrics, provide a visual guide to ensure that hems are straight and square by marking a line on the fabric with a pencil and pulling out a thread across the width.*

2 *Place the fabric right side down and fold over double ¾-in (2-cm) hems along each side and press. Pin the side hems in place.*

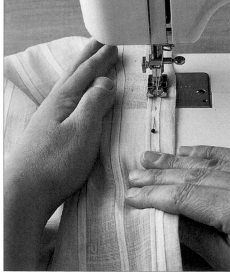

3 *Fold over a double 2-in (5-cm) hem at the base of the curtain, press, and pin the hem in place.*

4 *Machine-stitch the hems at each side of the curtain, making sure that the hems are even and the stitching straight.*

5 *Machine-stitch the base hem of the curtain, again making sure that the stitching is straight.*

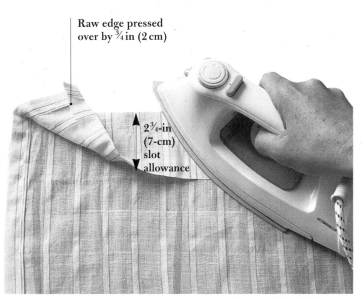

Raw edge pressed over by ¾ in (2 cm)

2¾-in (7-cm) slot allowance

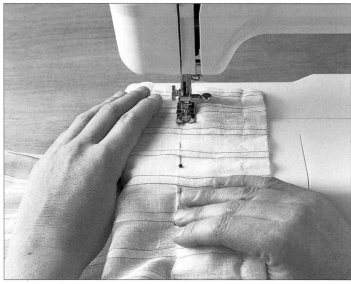

6 *At the top of the curtain, press over the raw edges ¾ in (2 cm). Then press over an additional amount for your slot allowance (see p. 48) and pin in position. The allowance here is 2¾ in (7 cm).*

7 *Machine-stitch along the top of the curtain ¾ in (2 cm) in from the edge and again along the base of the folded section to form the slot for the pole. Repeat steps 2–7 to make the second curtain, slot the curtains on the pole, and insert the pole into brackets (see p. 53).*

VARIATION ON UNLINED CURTAINS

Instead of a sheer fabric, a thick woolen blanket cloth was used for these curtains, providing a warm and cozy feel. Blanket cloth is a good fabric to use for unlined curtains since it is the same front and back. In place of a slot heading, these curtains have hooks attached to the back along the top (see p. 49) and they hang from rings on a plain wooden pole.

CONTRAST-LINED CURTAIN

I N MEDIEVAL TIMES heavy textile hangings were often draped across cold walls or doorways to keep out drafts. Most homes have efficient heating systems these days and little or no need for draft excluders. But this style of paneled curtain, supported on hand-sewn hooks, lends a touch of historic grandeur and elegance to your home.

The example shown here (opposite) is made from a width of heavy embroidered chenille and hangs from a solid wooden pole mounted above the doorway. The tasseled tieback gives the curtain shape and keeps it off the doorway for access. Since the curtain is seen from both sides we have lined it with an equally attractive plainer but contrasting chenille.

Type of window

• This curtain is not used over windows but within the house. It has two "fronts," both of which are on view.
• This type of double-sided curtain is also useful as a room divider. It does not have to extend across the entire room and can hang on a short pole projecting from a wall at right angles. You can use a heavy curtain hung in this way to break up a large area or create a backdrop for furniture.
• Part of a large landing or hallway can sometimes serve as a small room or additional work space. A double-sided curtain screens the space when needed, without the permanence of a door or a wall.

Type of fabric

• Heavy fabric is most effective for this type of curtain – and best for excluding drafts.
• Choose fabric and lining that work well together. But bear in mind that the rooms or spaces on each side of the curtain may be decorated in different colors or styles. The same pattern used in one color on one side and in another on the other can look very effective.
• Make sure that the fabrics you choose are alike in weight since they are sewn edge to edge. If one is much heavier, it will drag on the other.

Options

• Instead of the discreet heading shown in this example, try using chunky eyelets punched across the top of the curtain. Slot a pole through the eyelets. Alternatively, you can use tab or ribbon headings, but make sure they are strong enough to support the weight of the heavy curtain material.
• For added color and texture, you could make borders or edgings on one or both sides of the curtain.
• Look at different styles of tieback, such as silk ropes and tassels, curly wrought iron, or natural jute.

WHAT YOU WILL NEED

Main fabric for curtain

Width
Finished width of curtain (see pp. 38–39),
plus 1½ in (4 cm) for hems

Length
Finished drop of curtain (see pp. 38–39),
plus 1½ in (4 cm) for hems

Lining fabric for curtain

Width
As for main fabric

Length
As for main fabric

Accessories

Hooks
Finished width of curtain, divided by 8
(if working in inches) or 20 (if working
in centimeters), plus 1

Allow enough hooks for one at each corner
and one every 8 in (20 cm) across the curtain

Pole
At least 36 in (90 cm) wider than
doorway so that it extends at least
18 in (45 cm) on each side

Making the curtain

1 *Place the main fabric and lining on a flat surface with right sides together. Match the raw edges at each side and pin them together ¾ in (2 cm) in from the edge.*

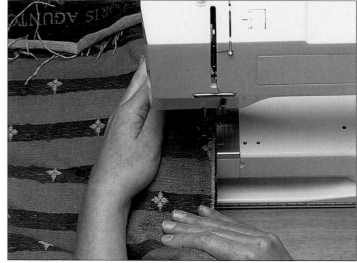

2 *Machine-stitch the main fabric and lining together at the sides, stopping ¾ in (2 cm) short of the top and base. Leave the top and base unstitched and turn the curtain right side out.*

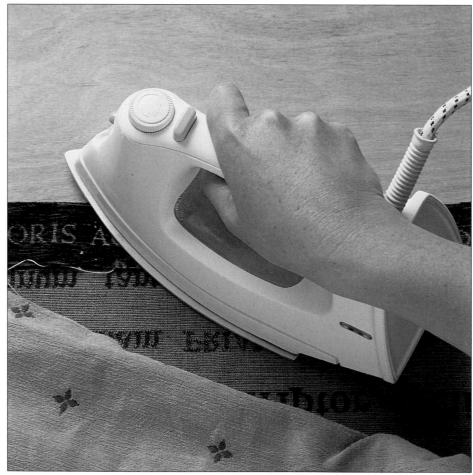

3 *Having pressed the side edges, making sure that the curtain aligns along the top and the pattern is straight on both sides, press under ¾-in (2-cm) hems at the top of the main fabric and lining. Press under hems at the base of the curtain in the same way, again making sure the pattern is straight.*

4 *Secure the main fabric and lining together at the top of the curtain using slipstitch (see p. 44). Repeat at the base.*

5 *Position hooks across curtain top on lining side, with one in each corner and the rest at 8-in (20-cm) intervals. Place them near the top, but not showing from the front. Stitch them in place by hand with couching stitch (see p. 45).*

6 *To attach the pole to the wall and hang the curtain, see instructions on p. 52. If you want to be able to pull the curtain back from the doorway, make sure that the final ring on one side is inside the wall bracket. If you want the curtain to remain always in the same position, covering the top of the doorway, keep the last ring outside the wall bracket as shown here (see right).*

VARIATIONS ON SIMPLE HEADINGS

Both of these curtains (see below) demonstrate how effective a simple approach can be. Like the contrast-lined curtain, they have headings without pleats or tape, even though they are made from much lighter fabrics. In place of hooks they are attached to their respective poles by ties knotted through small rings, allowing them to hang loosely. To add definition and form, each curtain has a border in the same fabric as the ties.

SINGLE CURTAIN WITH BOX PLEATS

ALLOW THE FABRIC TO SPEAK FOR ITSELF with this striking, unlined curtain. Despite a box-pleated heading, the curtain is essentially a panel that hangs from a simple wrought-iron pole. The heading, finished with a contrasting border in wool tartan, makes a flat, neat top but allows some fullness lower down the pleats, especially when the curtain is more than floorlength. The curtain is attached to the pole by hooks hand-sewn to the border, and the pole extends sufficiently to the side of the door so that the curtain can be pulled out of the way if necessary.

Type of window

• In some situations, a single curtain is more effective than a pair, such as on windows that abut walls or on single doors. A single curtain at each of a pair of windows helps to maximize light and is simpler than hanging two pairs.
• On a staircase where a tall window is set asymmetrically in the wall space, a single curtain covering part of the adjoining wall as well as the window helps to create a better visual balance in the area.
• Put box-pleated headings on view, not behind pelmets, but remember that they work best when flat across most of the top because they look less attractive when bunched up.

Type of fabric

• Choose a fabric that suits the tailored, disciplined look of this box-pleated curtain. Plain fabrics and simple stripes both work well.
• Avoid using a fabric with complex patterns that would look messy once pleated.
• Crisp fabrics, such as cotton and linen, pleat well and stay in pressed folds. Bulky or very soft fabrics do not, so are less suitable for this curtain.
• If the curtain is to be unlined, like the one shown here, use a fabric that looks good from both sides.

Options

• The box pleats shown here are folded edge to edge and are held in place by the border across the top. To create a different look, open out the heading by putting a space between each pleat.
• For a more dramatic curtain, you can make the spaces (or the pleats) in a contrasting fabric. Join strips of fabric together carefully before making the curtain and pressing the pleats in place.
• For a quick way of pleating, press the heading into pleats but do not stitch. Then, simply use clips to hold the pleats in place and fix the curtain to the pole.

WHAT YOU WILL NEED

Main fabric for curtain

Width
Finished width of curtain (see pp. 38–39), plus allowance for box pleats (see p. 40), plus 3 in (8 cm) for double side hems

Length
Finished drop of curtain (see pp. 38–39), plus 4 in (10 cm) for base hem and ¾ in (2 cm) for seam at the top

Fabric for contrasting border

Width
Finished width of curtain (see pp. 38–39), plus 2 in (5 cm) for seams

Length
Twice the finished border depth plus 1½ in (4 cm) for seams

Border shown here is 2 in (5 cm) wide

Accessories

Hooks
Finished width of curtain, divided by 6 (if working in inches) or 15 (if working in centimeters), plus 1

Curtain weights
1 for each corner, plus 1 for each width of fabric (see p. 43)

Pole
At least 36 in (90 cm) wider than doorway so that it extends at least 18 in (45 cm) on each side

Making the curtain

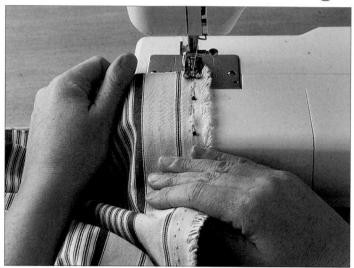

1 *When making wide unlined pleated curtains you will need to join fabric widths with French seams (see also p. 47). First place the two pieces of fabric wrong sides together, pin a ¾-in (2-cm) seam, and machine-stitch in place.*

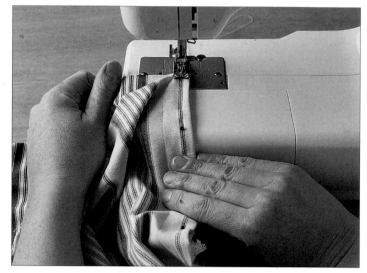

2 *Turn the fabric to the right side and press. Pin the right sides together so that the raw edges of the seam are concealed and the seam has a neat finish. Machine-stitch.*

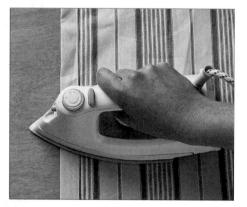

3 *With right side down, turn and press over a double ¾-in (2-cm) hem down both sides of the curtain.*

4 *Turn and press a double 2-in (5-cm) hem along the base of the curtain (see p. 46).*

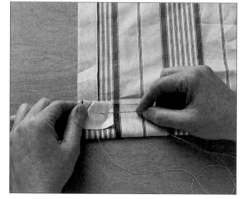

5 *Hand-sew a covered weight into each corner (see p. 46) and at the base of each of the seams joining fabric widths.*

6 *Pin both the side hems in place and secure them with machine stitching.*

7 *Machine-stitch the base hem, taking care not to run the needle over the covered weights inside the hem.*

Making the box pleats

1 *To mark positions of box pleats, measure in from one edge the width of one pleat front (see p. 51) and mark with a pin. Here, each pleat front is 4 in (10 cm) wide.*

2 *Measure from there the space allowed for fabric to be folded behind (double the width of pleat front) and mark with a pin. Here, the space is 8 in (20 cm).*

3 *Measure and mark width for next pleat front and then space allowed for fabric folded behind. Continue to repeat the process until you reach the other edge of the curtain. You will finish with a width for a pleat front.*

4 *To provide guides for folding the pleats, measure and mark with a pin the center spot between the first and second pin.*

5 *Measure and mark the center spot between the third and fourth pins in the same way and continue until you have measured and marked all of the widths of fabric to be folded behind.*

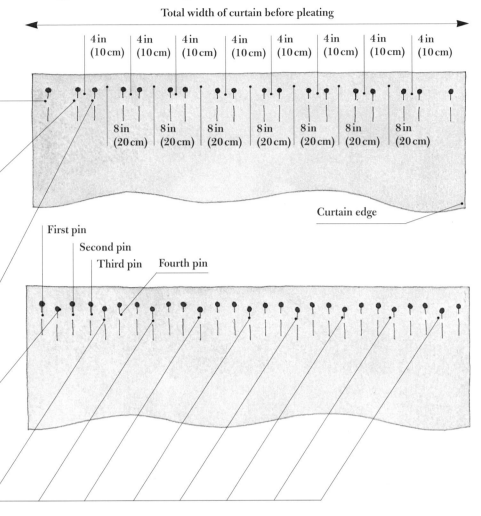

Total width of curtain before pleating

4 in (10 cm) 4 in (10 cm) 4 in (10 cm) 4 in (10 cm) 4 in (10 cm) 4 in (10 cm) 4 in (10 cm) 4 in (10 cm)

8 in (20 cm) 8 in (20 cm) 8 in (20 cm) 8 in (20 cm) 8 in (20 cm) 8 in (20 cm) 8 in (20 cm)

Curtain edge

First pin

Second pin

Third pin   Fourth pin

6 *Starting from one side, fold the fabric so that you bring the first pin to meet what is now the second pin (the pin that you inserted between the first and second pin in Step 4). Then bring what is now the third pin back to meet the second pin as well. Press the folds in place. Repeat to fold and press other pleats across the width of the curtain, folding the fabric so that what is now the fourth pin meets the fifth pin, the sixth meets the fifth, and so on.*

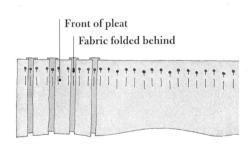

Front of pleat

Fabric folded behind

Attaching the border

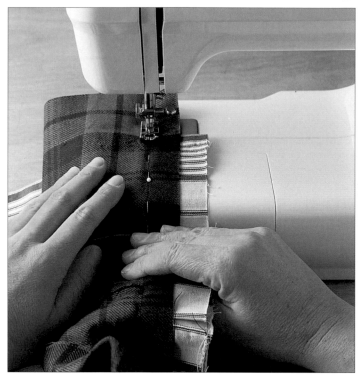

1 *With right sides together, place the contrasting border along the top of the curtain 1 in (2.5 cm) from the edge. Pin and machine-stitch along it 2 in (5 cm) from the top edge – 1 in (2.5 cm) down from the edge of the border. This attaches the border to the curtain and holds the pleats in place.*

Pin marking top of curtain

2 *Fold the border back over itself so that it covers the top of the curtain. Mark with pins the line of the top of the curtain (which is hidden underneath the border).*

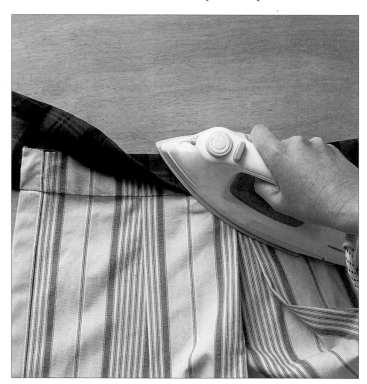

3 *Place the curtain right side down. Press the border over to the wrong side along the pinned foldline, pressing under the raw edge 1 in (2.5 cm) to form the hem.*

4 *Pin the border in place, turning under the raw edges at each end, and slipstitch (see p. 44) it to the back of the curtain.*

Attaching the hooks

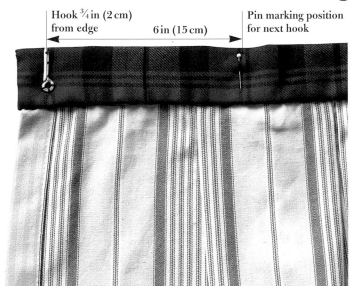

Hook ¾ in (2 cm) from edge   6 in (15 cm)   Pin marking position for next hook

1 *Position the first curtain hook ¾ in (2 cm) in from one end of the curtain. Place another hook ¾ in (2 cm) from the other end and use pins to mark the spaces for the remaining hooks in between. Allow about 6 in (15 cm) between each hook.*

2 *Use a couching stitch (see p. 45) to attach each of the hooks to the curtain securely, stitching through all layers of fabric in the border and the curtain. Put up the pole and hang the curtain (see p. 52).*

VARIATION ON CURTAIN WITH BOX PLEATS

The box pleats on these floor-length curtains are spaced out (see p. 40) to give a very different look. Instead of having a border and hooks at the top, they are attached to the pole with clips that also keep the pleats in position.

TARTAN LOOSE DRAPE

I F YOU HAVE AN INTERESTING window that you would like to make into a focal point, you can frame it with a length of unlined fabric that highlights this feature and shapes the view. The draped fabric is held by sewn rings, which fit over the stems of the rosettes fixed at the outermost points, and by a looped braid and tassel in the center. The fabric falls into shape under its own weight.

Type of window

• Tall, rather than wide, windows are best for this kind of fabric draping. The proportions of the window and drape need to be in harmony for this arrangement to work.
• Do not overload small windows – allow the "tails" of the fabric to fall only part way down each side, not to the floor.
• The drape does not close, so the window will be permanently on view. Bear this in mind both in terms of decor and of privacy and security.

Type of fabric

• Choose fabrics that are the same on both sides, such as this richly patterned wool tartan. Reversible fabrics are also suitable.

• Choose a fabric that drapes well and does not fall into stiff folds. The arrangement should be fluid, with the fabric doing all the work.

Options

• To give the drape a different look, use flat braids or ribbons in contrasting or harmonious colors to swag up the center of the drape. Loop them over a small hook and tie them in a knot, or sew the ends together around the fabric.

——— WHAT YOU WILL NEED ———

Fabric for drape
Width
About 27½ in (70 cm), plus 3 in (8 cm) for hems

Length
Twice finished drop (see pp. 38–39), plus distance between rosettes (usually width of window frame), plus 20 in (50 cm) to allow fabric to drape on floor, plus 3 in (8 cm) for hems

Accessories
Brass rings
3 brass rings up to ½ in (12 mm) diameter

Brass hook
1 for central ring

Rosettes
2

Making the drape

Press under and stitch double ¾-in (2-cm) hems all around the fabric. Mark the position of the rings on the fabric. Place one in the center and one at each side to match the position of the drape rosettes. Position the drape over the rosettes as shown opposite.

Finished drop of curtain – here, 107½ in (273 cm) – plus 10 in (25 cm) for draping on floor

Distance between rosettes – here, 95 in (241 cm)

Finished drop of curtain – here, 107½ in (273 cm) – plus 10 in (25 cm) for draping on floor

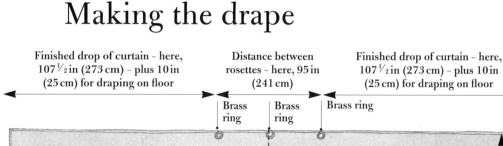

Brass ring

Brass ring

Brass ring

27½ in (70 cm)

¾-in (2-cm) double hem around all edges

Center of fabric

VARIATIONS ON TARTAN LOOSE DRAPE

Antique rosettes
Choose different styles and finishes of rosette to suit the fabric and other furnishings. Here, an antique rosette in wood perfectly complements the tartan fabric.

Contrast braid
A length of braid is looped around the center of the drape, pulling it into shape. The silky luster of the braid contrasts with the mat finish of the woolen tartan.

GATHERED CURTAINS

BAY WINDOWS can be difficult to curtain, mainly because their angles preclude the use of some types of headings. Poles can be used, but they usually have to be fitted in three sections and the brackets then interfere with the pulling of the curtains. Here a metal track, bent to fit the bay, is used to hold the curtains. A discreet cord and pulley mechanism allows the curtains to be pulled around the window. The track is a practical, not decorative, device and it is concealed by a lath and fascia covered in the same fabric as the curtains so that they blend in. The curtains are lined with a contrasting fabric and gathered onto a 1-in (2.5-cm) tape. Interlining adds extra warmth and fullness.

Type of window

• These curtains suit tall wide windows, allowing scope for fabrics with large patterns and more random designs, such as toile de Jouy, which work best over a wide expanse.

• They are useful where there is little room above the window for a pole, such as in a bay, or where the window is close to the ceiling. Bear in mind that metal curtain tracks need to be put up professionally since special tools are required for bending the track around corners.

• For full-length windows, continue curtains onto the floor instead of leaving them hovering just above it. This gives a more luxurious feel – and can help to overcome the problem of uneven floors or windows.

Type of fabric

• Almost any type of fabric can be used for these curtains. One advantage of corded tracks is that they allow the curtains to be pulled without being handled. This is useful for white curtains or curtains in fragile or antique fabrics that might become spoiled if pulled manually every day.

• Remember that large windows dominate a room so keep this in mind when choosing a fabric. An extremely bold pattern might be overpowering.

• Curtains of this type benefit from interlining. It makes the curtains more sumptuous and adds an insulating layer.

Options

• For additional interest, fit a holdback at each side to tuck the curtains behind. This gives shape to the way that the curtains frame the windows.

• Cover the lath and fascia in a fabric different from that of the curtains to make a feature of them. Or match the color of the walls to make them blend in.

WHAT YOU WILL NEED

Main fabric for each curtain and to cover lath and fascia

Width
Finished width of curtain (see pp. 38–39), plus allowance for gathering of heading tape (see p. 40), plus 4 in (10 cm) for side hems

Length
Finished drop of curtain (see pp. 38–39), plus 10 in (25 cm) for top and base hems

Fabric for lath and fascia
Enough fabric to cover lath and fascia completely

Lining fabric for each curtain

Width
As for main fabric

Length
As for main fabric

Interlining fabric for each curtain

Width
As for main fabric

Length
As for main fabric, less 4 in (10 cm)

Accessories

Tape
1-in (2.5-cm) tape cut to width of fabric, plus 2 in (5 cm) for finishing ends

Brass curtain hooks
1 for every 4 in (10 cm) of pulled-up tape, plus 1 at each end

Covered curtain weights
1 for each corner, plus 2 for each width

Track
Metal track that can be attached to the back of the fascia

If track needs to be curved as here, this requires special tools and so it is advisable to seek professional help

Lath
2 x 1-in (5 x 2.5-cm) lath cut to fit inside the bay

Fascia
2-in (5-cm) deep fascia cut to the same length as the lath

Attaching the interlining

When making a large lined and interlined curtain, it is best to spread the fabric across the worktable and stitch one width of fabric at a time (see pp. 38 and 42–43). The entire base hem is pressed into place first, then stitched to the end of the first width. At this point you should lock in the interlining (see p. 44) to the main fabric (see Step 2), before continuing to the next width.

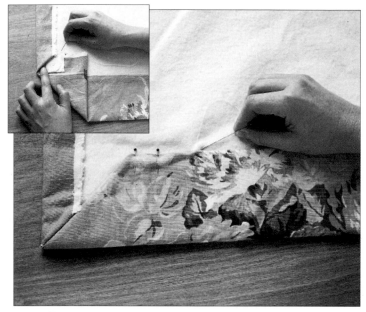

1 *Follow the instructions on p. 46 to attach the interlining to the back of the curtain with a double lining hem at the base and mitered corners. Insert covered weights (see inset and p. 46) into the base hem at the corners and at each half width.*

2 *As you work your way across the curtain, lock in (see p. 44) each width of interlining to the main fabric.*

Attaching the lining

1 *Take the contrast lining and turn and press a double 2-in (5-cm) hem along the base (see p. 46). Machine-stitch the base hem in place.*

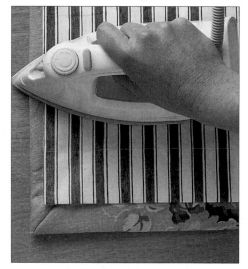

2 *Lay the lining on the curtain, wrong sides together, turning under the edges at the side hem, and press as shown. Position the lining so that it is about 1 in (2.5 cm) in from the edges of the curtain and pin in place.*

3 *Secure the lining fabric to the edge of the curtain at the left-hand side using slipstitch (see p. 44).*

4 *Lock in the lining across the curtain at width and half-width intervals (see p. 43).*

5 *Loosely secure the lining at the base hem at width and half-width intervals, using chain stitch (see p. 45) as shown. Finally, secure the lining to the edge of the curtain at the right-hand side, as in Step 3, p. 78.*

Attaching the heading tape

1 *Mark the finished dropline at the top of the curtain on the wrong side and press over the raw edge about 2 in (5 cm).*

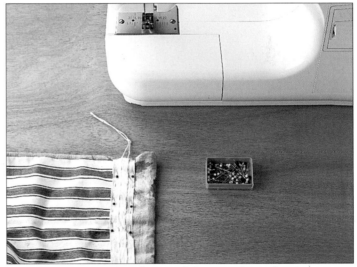

2 *Pin the tape across the top of the curtain so that it covers the raw edges of the curtain top and machine-stitch the tape in place.*

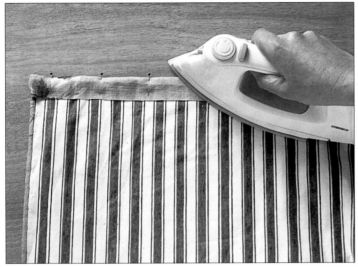

3 *Secure one end of the tape following the instructions on p. 48 and pull up the strings of the heading tape until the curtain is gathered to its required width. Make sure that the fullness is evenly distributed across the width.*

4 *Knot the strings of the tape, rolling the surplus into a bow shape, and stitch the strings to the tape (see inset). Cover the lath and fascia (see p. 56), attach the track, and hang the curtains.*

LINED CURTAINS WITH DRAPE

BOLD COLORS, combined in a classic arrangement, make these chenille curtains and slot-headed drape an eye-catching focal point for a room. The curtains have a pencil-pleat heading and are hung from a corded track that is fixed to the wall above the French doors and hidden behind the drape. They fall into soft undulating folds, which are held back by small metal pole finials attached to the frame of the doors.

The drape at the top slots over a pole made of the same material as the finials. Wide bands in a contrasting color loop the drape into shape, making a scoop that, at its deepest, is about one-sixth of the overall drop of the curtains. The track and pole are fitted close together in the wall above the window, as the curtains do not need to be drawn open or closed.

Type of window

• Full-length curtains with a pelmet or drape need tall, elegant windows. Here, the arrangement created by the held-back curtains and the scoop of the drape is contained within the shape of the French doors.

• These curtains and drape would also suit a single window or door or a matching pair of windows.

Type of fabric

• For a strong but simple look, use plain fabrics, with a striking color contrast between the drape and the curtains.
• Velvets, chenilles, or heavy wools are perfect for these curtains. They have the right texture and weight to drape well and retain the shape.
• Create an even more dramatic effect with a wide black and white stripe for the curtain and a narrower stripe for the drape, with contrast bands of burgundy or emerald.

Options

• Use a diagonal stripe or tapestry strip for the bands to add interest.
• For a more subtle arrangement, make both curtains and drape in one fabric, with just the bands at the top in a contrasting color.
• Move the contrast bands to the center to give a different shape to the base of the drape.

WHAT YOU WILL NEED: CURTAIN

Main fabric for each curtain

Width
Finished width of curtain (see pp. 38–39), plus allowance for gathering of taped heading (see p. 40), plus 4 in (10 cm) for side hems

Length
Finished drop of curtain (see pp. 38–39), plus 10 in (25 cm) for top and base hems

Lining fabric for each curtain

Width
As for main fabric

Length
As for main fabric, less 4 in (10 cm)

Accessories

3-in (7.5-cm) tape
Width of fabric, plus 2 in (5 cm) for turning

Brass curtain hooks
1 for every 4 in (10 cm) of pulled-up tape, plus 1 at each end

Covered curtain weights
1 for each corner, plus 1 for each width

Corded track
Finished width of curtain

WHAT YOU WILL NEED: DRAPE

Fabric for drape

Width
Finished width of drape, plus 3 in (8 cm) for hems

Length
Finished drop of drape (about one-sixth of total drop of curtain), plus 12 ¼ in (31 cm) for hems, plus depth needed for the slot according to the size of pole (see p. 40)

Fabric for each band and piping

Width
Twice finished width of band, plus ¾ in (2 cm) for seams
Width of band shown here is 2 ¼ in (6 cm)

Length
The length required, plus 1 ½ in (4 cm) for seams
Length of band shown here is 10 in (25 cm)

Piping
Joined 2-in (5-cm) wide bias-cut strips (see p. 47) the finished width of the drape, plus 1 ½ in (4 cm) for turning in raw ends

Accessories

Piping cord
Finished width of drape

Pole
Metal pole with finials the width of the window, plus at least 8 in (20 cm)

2 extra finials to act as holdbacks for the curtains

Making the curtain

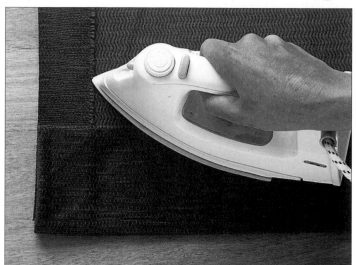

1 On the wrong side of the curtain, press over single 2-in (5-cm) side hems and a double 4-in (10-cm) base hem (see p. 46 for information on base hems).

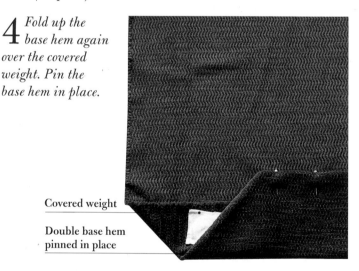

2 Fold back the side hems and fold back the base hem once. Secure the raw edge of the base hem with herringbone stitch (see p. 44).

3 Fold over the corner of the hem diagonally as shown, so that the pressed line of the side hem lines up with herringboned edge of the base hem. Insert a covered weight in what will be the finished corner and stitch in place.

4 Fold up the base hem again over the covered weight. Pin the base hem in place.

Covered weight

Double base hem pinned in place

5 Fold and press the side hem in again, forming a neat mitered corner, and pin it in place. Repeat Steps 3 to 5 to miter the corner at the other side of the curtain and then secure the side hems with herring-bone stitch, and the mitered corners and top of the base hem with slipstitch (see p. 44) as shown, inserting curtain weights at half-width intervals (see p. 43).

Side hem folded in

Mitered corner pinned in place

Attaching the lining

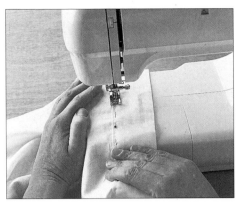

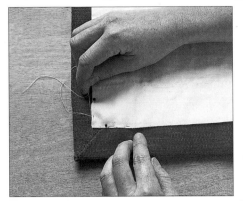

1 *Fold and machine-stitch a double 2-in (5-cm) base hem on the lining fabric (see p. 46).*

2 *Lay the lining on the back of the curtain, wrong sides together, so that it covers the curtain's stitched base and side hems. Press under the lining's raw edges by 1 in (2.5 cm) at the sides and slip-stitch it to the sides of the curtain as shown.*

3 *Fold back the lining at the base and loosely secure the top of the lining base hem to the top of the curtain base hem using chain stitch (see p. 45). Secure it at width and half-width intervals (see p. 43).*

Finishing the curtain

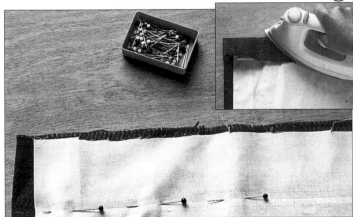

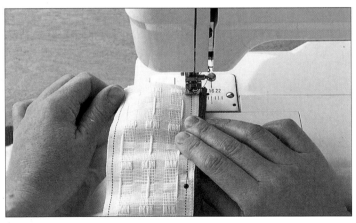

1 *Measure the finished drop from the base of the curtain and mark the finished dropline with pins at the top of the curtain on the wrong side. Fold over the raw edges 2 in (5 cm) at the top (see inset), press, and remove pins.*

2 *Pin the heading tape to the top of the curtain and machine-stitch top and bottom. Secure one end of tape by knotting the strings, folding tape under, and stitching across (see p. 48). This secures the strings and prevents them from unraveling.*

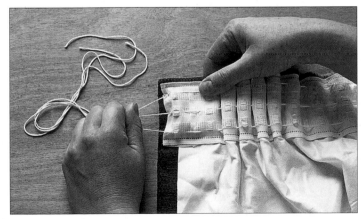

3 *Pull up the tape until the curtain is gathered to its finished width. Make sure that the gathering is evenly distributed across the width. Knot the strings of the tape.*

4 *Roll surplus strings up into a bow shape. Stitch the rolled-up strings firmly to heading tape. Repeat to make second curtain, insert hooks (see p. 48), and hang on track (see p. 53).*

Making the bands for the drape

Fabric folded in half lengthwise

Machine-stitch along pinned edge

Underside of band turned right side out

Seam pressed flat

1 *To make the two contrast bands, fold the fabric in half lengthwise, right sides together, and pin along the length ³⁄₈ in (1 cm) in from the edge. Machine-stitch along pinline.*

2 *Turn the fabric right side out and press so that seam lies in the center of the underside. Repeat to make the other band.*

Making the drape

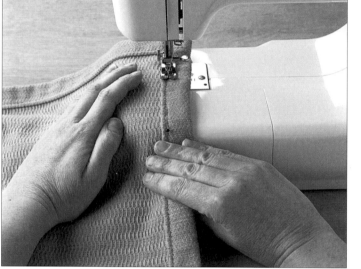

1 *Pin double ³⁄₄-in (2-cm) hems along the sides and base of the fabric for the drape. Machine-stitch the hems in place.*

2 *Measure, from the top of the fabric for the drape, the depth needed for the slot (see p. 40) and cut off this fabric. Put it aside until Step 1 of "Attaching the slot head to the drape," p. 85.*

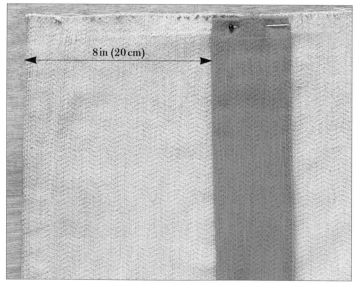

8 in (20 cm)

3 *Lay the rest of the fabric for the drape right side up and position the two bands on top of it, aligning the bands' raw edges with the top of the drape section and about 8 in (20 cm) in from each edge. Pin in place.*

4 *Place the made-up piping (see p. 47) along the top of the drape section. Machine-stitch the piping to the drape, sewing over the contrast bands to secure them.*

Attaching the slot head to the drape

1 *Place the slot fabric (see Step 2 of "Making the drape," p. 84) along top of drape, right sides together. Machine-stitch the slot to the drape, stitching over the bands and the edges of the piping.*

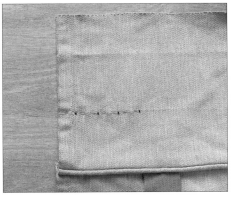

2 *Open out the slot and mark the fold-line, which will be the top of the drape, with pins.*

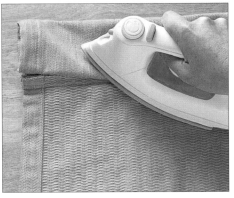

3 *Press over the slot section to the wrong side of the drape along the foldline, turning under the raw edge by ¾ in (2 cm).*

4 *Pin the slot in place so that it covers the seam as shown and secure it with slipstitch (see p. 44).*

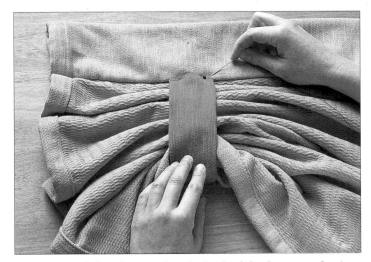

5 *Take each band around to the back of the drape, gathering the drape up at the same time. When the band is the required length, turn in the raw edge and slipstitch the end of the band to the back of the drape, beneath the slot.*

6 *Hang the curtain from a track and slot the drape onto a pole fitted close to the track. The two have to be close together for the arrangement to work. Before attaching the holdbacks for the curtains (see below), experiment by holding the curtain back by hand to see at what height the draping works to best effect.*

STRIPED CURTAINS

THESE EYE-CATCHING single curtains are made from strips of fabric sewn together, with alternating dark blue and dark green strips set between strips of cream. Across the top they have a wide slot heading made of the same fabrics, but stitched together in a contrasting order. Edging each curtain and dividing the slot at the top from the main section, is a length of piping in brilliant emerald green. This catches the light and contrasts with the mat surface of the rest of the fabric.

These curtains are intended to hang simply from their poles as flat panels. Rather than being drawn, the curtains are held in shape by cream rope and tassel tiebacks that keep them off the windows.

Type of window

• These curtains work well on either tall or short windows. Bear in mind that they do not draw across the top.

• It is important that single curtains look deliberate, not accidental. Fill the spaces between a pair of windows with pictures and make a feature of the way the curtains are hung with tiebacks.

Type of fabric

• The fabric used here is a crisp, stiff cotton. It is glazed but used on the reverse side. Plain colors, such as these, look best, but they can be either close to each other in tone or contrasting in color for a dramatic effect.

• Fabrics for the strips need to be of the same type or there is a danger of tension and stretching. Seams must stay flat inside the curtains, so avoid fabric that is bulky or that may fray.

Options

• For an understated, minimalist look, try using two fabrics that are close in color, such as creams or off-white cottons or linens.

• For a less dramatic look, alter the width of stripe, but remember that the narrower the stripes the more work there is. Try offsetting the main stripes with colors other than cream.

WHAT YOU WILL NEED

Main fabric for each curtain and slot heading

To calculate amount of stripes needed for each curtain, divide finished width of curtain by finished width of each stripe – here, 40 in (100 cm) divided by 4 in (10 cm), making 10 stripes

Width for curtain
For each stripe: finished width of curtain (see pp. 38–39), divided by number of stripes, plus 1½ in (4 cm) for side hems

Length for curtain
For each stripe: finished drop of curtain (see pp. 38–39), minus finished drop of slot heading, plus 8¾ in (22 cm) for base hem and top seam

Width for slot heading
For each stripe: finished width of curtain, divided by number of stripes, plus 1½ in (4 cm) for side hems

Length for slot heading
For each stripe: twice the finished drop of slot heading (see p. 40), plus 1½ in (4 cm) for hems

Slot heading on this curtain has a drop of 10 in (25 cm)

Lining and piping fabric for each curtain

Width for lining
Finished width of curtain, plus 1 in (2.5 cm) for side hems

Length for lining
Finished drop of curtain, plus twice finished drop of slot heading, plus 4¾ in (12 cm) for base hem and top seams

Piping fabric
Joined 2-in (5-cm) wide bias-cut strips (see p. 47): one piece finished width of curtain, plus twice the finished drop; 2 pieces each finished drop of slot heading, plus ¾ in (2 cm)

Accessories

Piping cord
As for piping fabric

Pole
The width of the window frame plus however much you want it to extend on either side (see p. 52)

Tiebacks
1 for each curtain

Making the curtain

1 *Lay out the cut strips for the first curtain in the desired order and, with right sides and ¾-in (2-cm) seams together, machine-stitch each strip to the next along the long edges to make the main curtain.*

2 *Fold over the seams to the center of each dark stripe so they do not show through the lighter stripes and press.*

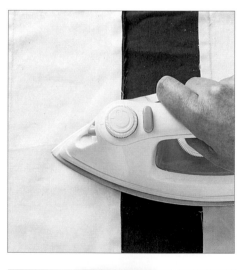

3 *Fold over a double 4-in (10-cm) hem at the base of the curtain and press (see p. 46 for more details on base hems).*

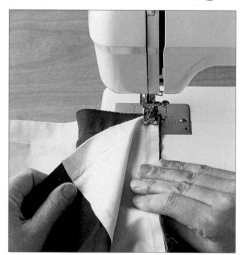

4 *Pin the hem in place and secure it with herringbone stitch (see p. 44). Repeat Steps 1 and 2 to make the slot heading, joining strips so the dark strips on the slot-line up with the light ones on the main curtain.*

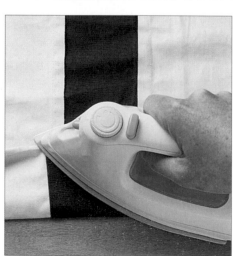

Attaching the piping and slot

1 *With curtain right side up, pin and machine-stitch made-up piping (see p. 47) to both sides of curtain and across top. Attach piping to sides only of slot heading.*

2 *Place the slot heading over piping at top of curtain, right sides together. Machine-stitch beside piping line, allowing a ¾-in (2-cm) seam.*

Main curtain

Slot heading

Finishing the curtain

1 *Having pressed and stitched a double 2-in (5-cm) base hem on lining, place lining on back of curtain, pressing under raw edges close to piping. Slipstitch (see p. 44) in place along base and sides.*

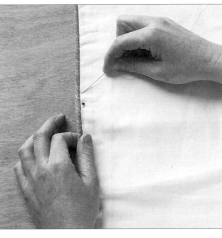

2 *At the top of the curtain, fold the heading section over to make the slot. Press under the raw edge.*

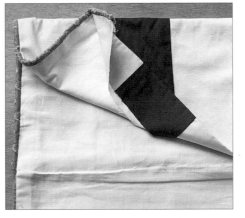

3 *Secure the lower edge of the slot heading section with slip-stitch. Repeat the whole process to make the second curtain. Put up the poles and hang the curtains (see p. 52).*

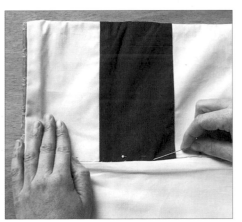

VARIATION ON STRIPED CURTAIN

This curtain demonstrates a wonderfully creative use of fabric. Long strips made up of squares and rectangles of colored silk are inset between sections of green velvet. The effect resembles a stylish patchwork and has a far less formal feel than the regimented stripes of the main project.

CURTAIN WITH SELF-PELMET

A WINDOW IN THE CORNER of a landing can be difficult to curtain successfully. This single self-pelmet curtain, set into the corner on one side and balanced visually by furniture and a wall light on the other, provides an elegant solution.

The fringed self-pelmet makes the curtain smart without being overly formal. Long goblet pleats are set into the top of the curtain, which has been folded down to give the impression of being a separate pelmet. The fringe, which is hand-sewn to the base of the self-pelmet, adds texture and helps define the two sections of the curtain.

Type of window

• This type of curtain looks best on tall windows that are longer than they are wide.
• If space permits, fit the pole from which the curtain hangs above the window. This has the effect of lengthening the curtain and uses the space above the window. The width of the heading should not extend beyond the window frame and the curtain should hang to the floor.

Type of fabric

• Damasks, brocades, and tapestries would be excellent fabrics for this curtain, which lends itself to period settings.

While these may be first choices, this curtain could be made in almost any kind of fabric.
• Choose a fringe and tieback that complement the main fabric color rather than contrasting with it. Fringes can be dyed to match fabrics if necessary.
• If you are using a lighter fabric you can add interlining (see p. 46), but with heavy fabrics, such as the one used here, this is probably not necessary.

Options

• Make a fabric skirt to hang in front at the top of the curtain. The two are held together by one line of eyelets through which a pole can thread. Add a border to the skirt to give definition.
• Try a casual arrangement with fabric draped behind and over a pole to look like a full-length curtain with a short pelmet drape above.
• Dispense with the self-pelmet and go for a simpler approach with no fringe.
• Double the impact by making two identical curtains and using them on a pair of matching windows. Tie one back to the right and one to the left to create an overall symmetrical effect. You could even use this style on a row of three windows, tying them all back in the same direction.

WHAT YOU WILL NEED

Main fabric for curtain

Width

Finished width of curtain (see pp. 38–39), plus 7 in (18 cm) for each pleat (see p. 40), plus 4 in (10 cm) for side hems

Length

Finished drop of curtain (see pp. 38–39), plus 8¾ in (22 cm) for top and base hems, plus twice the depth of self-pelmet

Depth of the self-pelmet shown here is 10 in (25 cm)

Lining and fringe fabric for curtain

Width for lining

As for main fabric

Length for lining

As for main fabric, less 4 in (10 cm) per drop

Fringe

As cut width for main fabric, plus 1½ in (4 cm) for finishing raw ends

Accessories

Pin hooks

As number of pleats, plus 2

Curtain weights

2 for each width of fabric (see p. 43)

Pole

Width of window frame, plus removable finials (so that one end buts wall)

Making the curtain

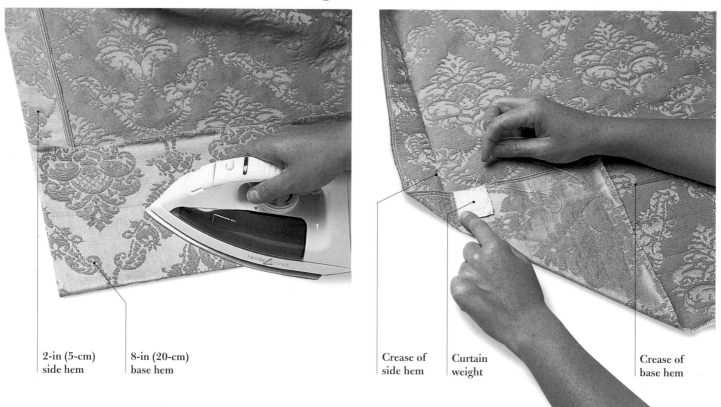

2-in (5-cm) side hem   8-in (20-cm) base hem

Crease of side hem   Curtain weight   Crease of base hem

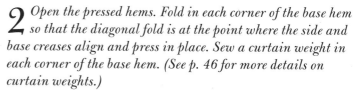

1 *Place the main fabric right side down and press over 2-in (5-cm) hems on each side. Fold over an 8-in (20-cm) hem at the base of the curtain and press.*

2 *Open the pressed hems. Fold in each corner of the base hem so that the diagonal fold is at the point where the side and base creases align and press in place. Sew a curtain weight in each corner of the base hem. (See p. 46 for more details on curtain weights.)*

Double hem at base

Mitered corner

3 *Press the base hem over 4 in (10 cm) twice to form a double 4-in (10-cm) hem. Fold the side hem in to form a neat mitered corner. Press and secure the corner with slipstitch (see p. 44). Repeat on the other corner of the base hem.*

4 *Secure both of the side hems of the curtain with herringbone stitch (see p. 44).*

5 *Once both side hems are stitched in place, secure the base hem of the curtain with slipstitch.*

Attaching the lining

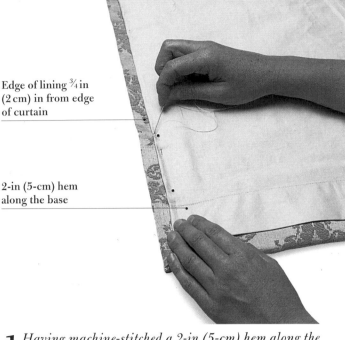

Edge of lining ¾ in (2 cm) in from edge of curtain

2-in (5-cm) hem along the base

1 *Having machine-stitched a 2-in (5-cm) hem along the base, press over 2-in (5-cm) hems on each side of the lining. Position the lining on the curtain, wrong sides together, with edges of the lining ¾ in (2 cm) in from edges of the curtain. Pin in place and slipstitch (see p. 44) sides of lining to the fabric.*

2 *Secure the underside of the base hem of the lining to the base hem of the curtain by hand, using chain stitch (see p. 45).*

Making the self-pelmet

1 *At the top of the curtain, press over the lining and fabric to make a ¾-in (2-cm) hem on the lining side of the curtain.*

2 *Fold the curtain over to the right side to twice the depth of the finished self-pelmet. Fold up again so that the edge with the pressed hem aligns with the fold at the top of the curtain. Pin in place.*

3 *Secure the top of the curtain with slipstitch. Take care to stitch through all layers of the curtain and self-pelmet so the folded section stays in place.*

4 *Lay the length of fringe along the unstitched folded edge of the self-pelmet. Stitch the fringe in place along the fold so that it hangs below the pelmet. Stitch the fringe to the pelmet fold only, not through all layers of fabric.*

5 *Pin the ends of the pelmet section in place, tucking in the raw ends of the fringe as you do so. Secure the ends of the pelmet with slipstitch (see p. 44).*

Making up the goblet pleats

Spacing your pleats

To work out how much space you have between each pleat, first subtract 8 in (20 cm) from the curtain's width to allow for 4 in (10 cm) of unpleated area at each edge. Multiply the number of pleats you want by 7 in (18 cm) and also subtract this total from the width. Finally, divide the resulting sum by the number of spaces you need between the pleats (the number of pleats minus 1).

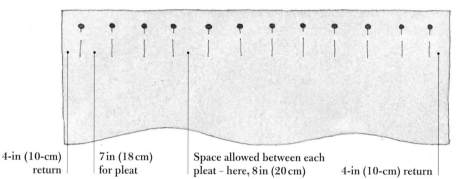

4-in (10-cm) return   7 in (18 cm) for pleat   Space allowed between each pleat – here, 8 in (20 cm)   4-in (10-cm) return

Pin 4 in (10 cm) from edge

Pin another 7 in (18 cm) from edge

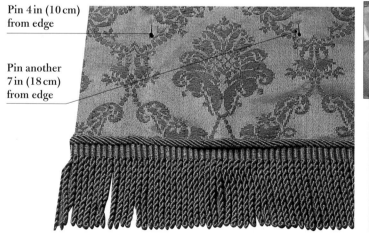

1 *Measure 4 in (10 cm) in from one edge and mark with a pin. Measure and mark another 7 in (18 cm) for the first pleat and then do the same for the amount of space to be left between each pleat (see diagram above). Continue to measure and mark alternately the allowance for the pleats and for the space in between until, after the last pleat, you are 4 in (10 cm) from the other side.*

2 *To make a pleat, fold back the first pin to meet the second pin, wrong sides together (see inset). Machine-stitch along the line of the pins through all layers down to and over the top of the fringe.*

3 Fold back the third pin to meet the fourth and repeat the process until you have folded and stitched all of the pleats. Open them out.

4 On the back of the curtain, insert a pin hook on the stitched line of each pleat and at each end beyond the pleats. Hang the curtain (see p. 52) and attach the tieback.

VARIATIONS ON CURTAIN WITH SELF-PELMET

Curtain with self-pelmet, border, and ties
This pelmet is simply an extra length of fabric that was added to the top of the finished drop and folded forward so that it falls in front of the curtain. The curtain is held to the pole by ties attached to the top (see p. 17). A perimeter border, made in the same contrasting fabric as the ties, adds definition.

Unsewn curtains with self-pelmet
These curtains are simplicity itself and show how effectively fabric can be used with little or no sewing. The two pieces of striped fabric were cut to the right width and length and then slung over a curtain wire. The folded section at the top of each curtain creates a practical and visual balance.

PLAIN ROMAN SHADE

THE APPEAL of Roman shades lies in their simplicity and the economical use they make of both fabric and window space. They are little more than panels of fabric that lie flat against the window when down and have a simple cording mechanism that allows them to be raised in a series of simple folds.

The cording mechanism works with the help of a number of thin wooden battens called dowel rods. Rods are attached to the lining and run horizontally across the back of the shade at regular intervals. The shade is supported on a lath hung across the top of the window, and the cord runs up through a series of rings attached to the rods in the center and at each side of the shade up to the lath at the top. The cords then run across to one side of the shade where they are secured to a drop weight.

Type of window

• Roman shades suit almost any type of window and many different styles of room. This type of shade fits neatly within or close to the framed shape of the window and does not detract from the window's own architectural or decorative features.
• They are particularly useful where there is no room for curtains to hang at either side of a window and where you want a clean, uncluttered look.

• This style of shade is not suitable for windows more than 5 ft (1.5 m) wide. Shades any wider than this are difficult to maneuver, but you can get around this by using a row of shades.

Type of fabric

• Follow the shade's strong, vertical shape and choose simple stripes or checks, or a strong pattern that is not lost when the shade is folded up. Avoid anything that is too fussy or busy.
• Choose a fabric that will keep its shape when folded. Crisp cottons are easiest to work with, but heavy wool tartan or even fine muslin also work well.

Options

• A shade made in a strong color or pattern stands out, especially against paler walls. If the shade is made in a plain fabric similar in color to the surrounding walls, it merges and takes on an architectural quality.
• To add interest at the top of the shade, attach a strip of the same or contrasting fabric to the lath at the top to make a false pelmet.
• Add borders or insets in contrasting colors or fabrics to provide more interest or pick up a color that appears elsewhere in the room.

WHAT YOU WILL NEED

Main fabric for shade

Width
Finished width of shade (see pp. 38–39), plus 4 in (10 cm) for side hems

Length
Finished drop of shade (see pp. 38–39), plus 2 in (5 cm) for the base hem, plus 10 in (25 cm) for attaching the top to the lath

Lining fabric for shade and rod pockets

Width for lining
As for main fabric

Length for lining
As for main fabric

Width for each rod pocket
4¾ in (12 cm)

Length for each rod pocket
Finished width of shade, plus 1½ in (4 cm)

Accessories

Dowel rods
As number of rod pockets cut to the finished width of shade

Lath
2 x 1-in (5 x 2.5-cm) timber lath cut to the finished width of shade

Brass rings
As number of rod pockets, multiplied by 3

Screw eyes
As number of rows of rings, plus 1

Polyester cord
Enough for twice the drop of the shade, plus the width, multiplied by the number of rows of rings (see p. 54)

Brass drop weight and cleat

Making the shade

1 *Lay the fabric for the shade right side down. Fold over and press 2-in (5-cm) hems down each side and at the base. Make sure that the corners are square.*

Square corner

2 *Unfold the pressed hems and turn in each corner so that the diagonal fold is at the point where side and base creases intersect. Press the corners.*

Crease along side

Crease along base

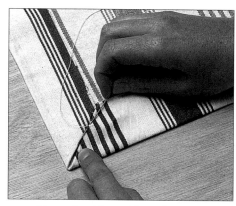

3 *Turn the side and base hems in again so that the folds meet. Stitch them together by hand, using slipstitch (see p. 44). Repeat at the other corner.*

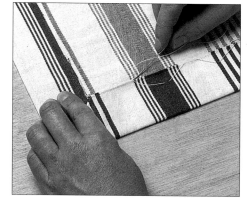

4 *Secure the sides and base hem of the shade with herringbone stitch (see p. 44).*

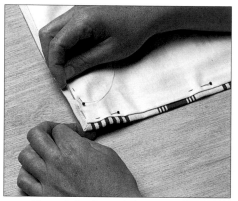

5 *Press 2-in (5-cm) hems on the side and base of the lining. Pin and slipstitch it onto the shade, wrong sides together, so that about ³⁄₈ in (1 cm) of the shade's hem shows beyond the lining.*

Making the rod pockets

1 *Take the fabric for one rod pocket and fold it in half lengthwise, wrong sides together. Turn over the long raw edges ³⁄₈ in (1 cm) to form a hem and press.*

2 *Turn over the same long edge by ³⁄₈ in (1 cm) again to form a double hem. Press and machine-stitch the double hem in place.*

3 *At one end, fold the raw edges over twice to form a double ³⁄₈-in (1-cm) hem. Press and machine-stitch this hem in place as well. Repeat to make other pockets.*

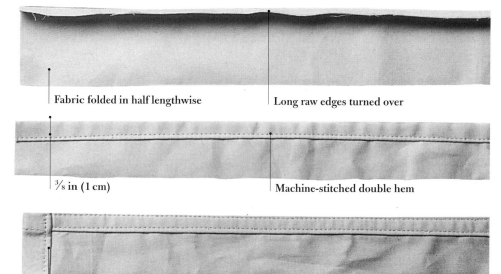

Fabric folded in half lengthwise

Long raw edges turned over

³⁄₈ in (1 cm)

Machine-stitched double hem

Machine-stitched double hem at end

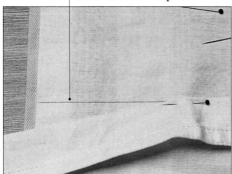

Position marked in pencil

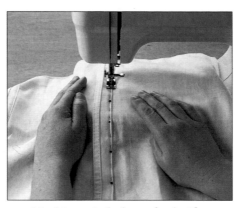

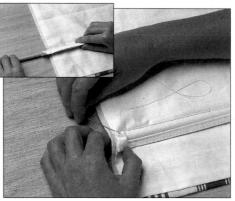

4 *Mark the position of the rod pockets (see p. 54) onto the back of the shade in pencil. Pin each pocket into place along its folded edge to align with the pencil marks.*

5 *Machine-stitch the pocket in place through all layers, keeping close to the folded edge.*

6 *After inserting a dowel rod into the pocket (see inset), finish the open end by turning in a double ⅜-in (1-cm) hem and securing with slipstitch (see p. 44). Repeat to make remaining pockets.*

Cording the shade

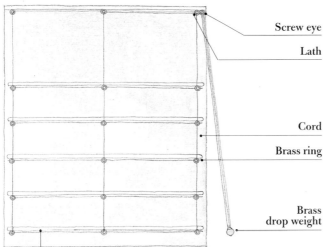

Screw eye

Lath

Cord

Brass ring

Brass drop weight

Rod pocket with rod inside

1 *Couch-stitch (see p. 45) three brass rings to each pocket – one at each end, just in from the side, and one in the center (see diagram).*

2 *Fix the lath to the top of the shade following the instructions on p. 55.*

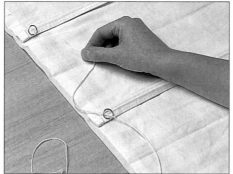

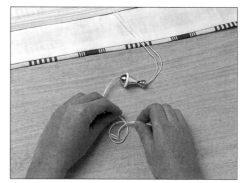

3 *Make sure the fabric is hanging completely straight and screw three screw eyes through the fabric into the lath on the back side. Attach one in line with each of the rows of brass rings and attach another one just in from the edge of the lath on the side where the pull strings will be (see pp. 54–55).*

4 *Tie one length of white cord to the ring in the bottom left-hand corner. Thread it up through the row of rings and the screw eye at the top and then along the top through the remaining screw eyes. Leave a loose end of cord the same length as the shade. Take cords through the other rows of rings in the same way (see diagram and p. 54).*

5 *With the shade unfolded, make sure that all the cords are straight and that all the loose ends are the same length. Thread the loose ends of the cords through a brass drop weight and secure with a tight knot so they do not slip through. Trim the ends of the cords and fix the shade in position (see pp. 56–57).*

ROLLED SHADE WITH TIES

THE BEAUTY OF THIS elegant shade lies in its simplicity. It uses fabric in its most unstructured form, falling naturally from its support. Since it does not have a cording system, this shade is decorative rather than functional. To operate it, you simply roll up the lower part of the shade to the desired position from the base and then hold it in place with ties, which are made here in an attractive contrasting fabric.

The shade is made so that some of the front fabric is taken around to the back of the shade at its base. This ensures that no lining fabric is visible when the shade is rolled up. At the top of the shade is a simple slot or sleeve for the pole support.

Type of window

• This style of shade is excellent for a window that is not very attractive or that looks onto an unappealing view. The shade can be kept half lowered, as here, held in place by the knotted ties.

• Tall, rectangular sash or casement windows are suitable for this simple shade.

• There must be enough space above the window casement for a pole to be fitted so that the fabric falls outside and in front of the window.

• It is a useful shade for situations such as a staircase window, where the shade is decorative and does not need to be raised and lowered regularly.

Type of fabric

• The silk taffeta used here is the perfect fabric for this shade. It is not heavy, but stays in place when rolled up and shimmers against the light.

• Alternatively, use any fabric that keeps its shape when rolled. Since so much of the fabric is visible most of the time, a bold, large-scale pattern can be used successfully.

• The ties should provide a strong visual contrast, so choose the fabric accordingly. In this example, boldly colored silk taffetas are used for both the shade and the ties, but the different scale of check and the strong color contrast adds interest and drama to the finished look.

Options

• Instead of slotting the shade onto a pole, try hanging it with special clips that loop the pole and grip the fabric. Many types of decorative clips are available, but they are only strong enough to hold lightweight fabric, such as silk taffeta (see variation on p. 103).

• For a more solid country look, use a bare wooden pole instead of the slender metal pole shown here. Or, paint a pole to match the fabric you choose for the shade or other colors in the room.

• Try making the shade and ties in strongly contrasting fabrics to create a different look. For example, use rough linen for the shade and make ties in velvet, or try a plain bleached sailcloth with hessian ties.

WHAT YOU WILL NEED

Main fabric for shade

Width

Finished width of shade (see pp. 38–39), plus 4 in (10 cm) for side hem allowances

Length

Finished drop of shade (see pp. 38–39), plus 20 in (50 cm) to go around to the back of the shade, plus 1½ in (4 cm) for hem allowances, plus allowance for slot at the top (see p. 41)

Lining fabric for shade

Width

As for main fabric

Length

As for main fabric, less 40 in (100 cm)

Accessories

Ties

For each tie, a 4¾-in (12-cm) wide strip twice the finished drop of the shade, plus 40 in (100 cm), plus ¾ in (2 cm) for hem allowances

Pole

At least 18 in (45 cm) wider than the window frame so that it extends at least 9 in (22.5 cm) on each side

Making the shade

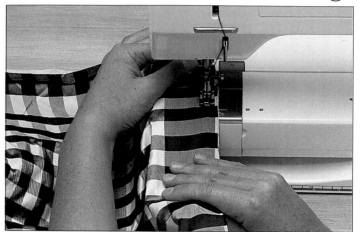

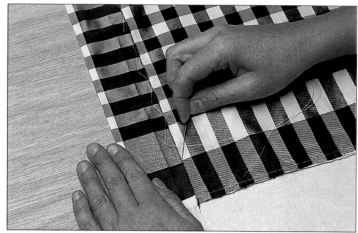

1 *Place the main shade fabric and lining right sides together, aligning the raw edges along the sides and the base. Machine-stitch along the base about ¾ in (2 cm) from the raw edges.*

2 *Open out fabric and lining and place flat, wrong side up. Press over 2-in (5-cm) hems on both sides of fabric and lining. Secure fabric hems only with herringbone stitch (see p. 44).*

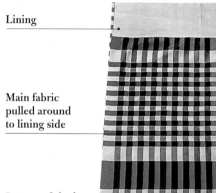

Lining

Main fabric pulled around to lining side

Bottom of shade

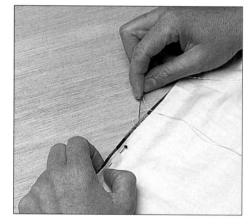

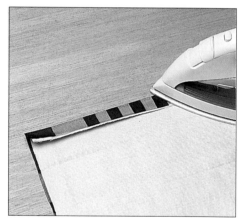

3 *Bring lining over the main fabric, wrong sides together, matching raw edges at the top. This pulls about 20 in (50 cm) of the main fabric around to the lining side.*

4 *Pin the lining to the shade at each side and slipstitch (see p. 44) together. Continue down the sides of the shade, stitching the sections of fabric together.*

5 *Fold over the raw edges at the top of the shade ¾ in (2 cm) and press.*

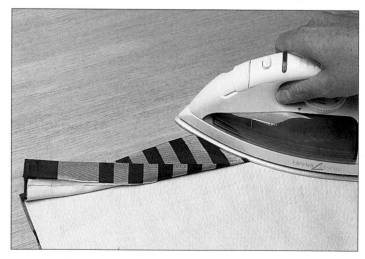

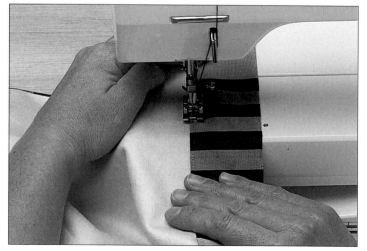

6 *Press over the top again to form the slot for the pole. The size of the slot depends on the size of pole used. Check the pole first with a scrap of fabric to help you work out the slot size. Make the slot big enough to allow the pole to move freely.*

7 *Once the size of the slot is correct, machine-stitch along the base of the hem of the slot.*

Making the ties

Tie folded in half lengthwise

Raw edge

Machine stitching along top

Back side of finished tie

Raw edges pressed and slipstitched

Seam running down center of back side

1 *Take fabric for one tie and fold in half lengthwise, right sides together. Machine-stitch close to the raw edges on the open long side only. Turn the tie right side out. Press the seam so that it lies in the center of the back side of the tie and will be hidden from sight when sewn to the shade. Press under raw edges at each end of the tie and slipstitch. Repeat to make the other tie.*

2 *Fold one tie in half widthwise. Stitch center fold to top of the shade, 8 in (20 cm) from left edge, so one half falls to the front of the shade and the other to the back. Repeat with second tie and stitch 8 in (20 cm) from right edge. Put up the pole (see p. 52) and hang the shade, then roll up the fabric base to the required height and knot the ties.*

VARIATION ON ROLLED SHADE WITH TIES

If the fabric of the shade is not too heavy – this silk taffeta is as light as could be – it can be held onto the pole with decorative clips. The clips, which are available in many different designs and finishes, loop over the pole and clip to the edge of the fabric. Make the shade without a slot to use in this way, or simply remove it from the pole and clip it up, as shown here. This makes a neat and simple change in the look which obscures the stitch-line of the slot. The clips used here are metal and can be painted to match the fabric color.

LINED PANEL SHADE

ALTHOUGH MADE IN a way similar to that of a Roman shade, this lined, slot-headed shade has a softer look – it does not have the series of rods and pockets that make the Roman shade so crisp and tailored. When pulled up, this shade falls into deep sculptural folds, which remain even when it is fully lowered.

To prevent the shade from pulling toward the center, one rod is fixed near the base in a pocket running between the two rows of rings. This also helps to keep the sides of the shade vertical. The rows of rings on the back for the cording mechanism are set a little in from both edges to give the shade its "tailed" sides. The deep contrast border along the base emphasizes the scooped shape of the shade, while narrower borders give definition to the sides.

To give it greater impact, the shade is hung so that it extends above and to each side of the window. Chunky wooden finials and brass brackets attaching the pole to the wall add texture and visual interest.

Type of window

• Single windows with space around them in rooms, halls, or stairways suit this kind of shade. Make sure there is enough room for the pole.

• Because of its shape and dramatic style, this bordered shade is best used on its own. It would not work well in combination with a curtain.

Type of fabric

• Use a fairly weighty fabric so the folds form without being too sharp or crisp. When raised, the shade should have a casual effect. Indian cottons, as shown here, chenilles, and tartans are all excellent choices for this shade.

• For a more opulent shade, use shimmery velvets – try canary yellow borders on a deep olive green shade. Heavy, tactile fabrics give the shade a cozy look, but it could also be made in more summery fabrics.

Options

• Experiment with different types of finial to suit your room – wrought iron, glass, or painted wood, for example. The pole itself is not visible once the shade is fitted, so the finials can be of different material.

• To alter the shape of the shade slightly, bring the rows of rings farther in from the edges. This will deepen the "tails" and emphasize the shape of the shade still more. Make sure the central "scoop" still covers the window.

— WHAT YOU WILL NEED —

Main fabric for shade

Width

Finished width of shade (see pp. 38–39), less the width of side borders, plus 1½ in (4 cm) for side hems

Length

Finished drop of shade (see pp. 38–39), less depth of base border, plus allowance for slot according to size of pole being used (see p. 41), plus 1½ in (4 cm) for top and base hems

Border fabric for shade

Width of side borders

Twice the finished border width, plus 1½ in (4 cm) for side hems

Width of side borders shown here is 2 in (5 cm)

Length of side borders

Finished drop of shade, plus allowance for slot according to size of pole being used (see p. 41), plus 1½ in (4 cm) for hems

Width of base border

Finished border width, plus 1½ in (4 cm) for hems

Width of base border shown here is 6 in (15 cm)

Length of base border

Width of shade, plus twice the cut width of side borders

Lining fabric for shade and rod pocket

Width for main lining

As for main fabric

Length

As for main fabric

Rod pocket

A 4¾-in (12-cm) wide strip of lining the width of the shade between the rings (see p. 54), plus 1½ in (4 cm) for seam allowances

Accessories

Brass rings

Finished drop of the shade, divided by 6 (if working in inches) or 15 (if working in centimeters), multiplied by 2

Screw eyes

3

Dowel rod

Width of shade between rings

Polyester cord

Enough for twice the drop of the shade, plus the width, multiplied by the number of rows of rings (see p. 54)

Pole

At least 12 in (30 cm) longer than the width of the window

Brass drop weight and cleat

Making the shade

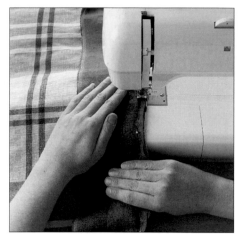

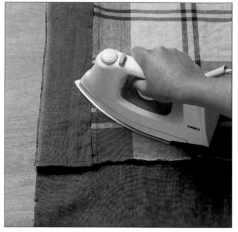

1 *With right sides together, pin and machine-stitch the side border fabric strips to the sides of the main fabric.*

2 *Pin the base border in place, running it across the side borders, and machine-stitch.*

3 *With shade right side down, press raw edges of seams at sides and base of the shade toward the borders.*

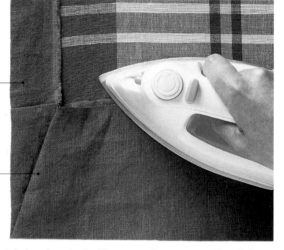

Side border folded in half to wrong side

Base border folded in with outer edges folded in diagonally

4 *Press the side borders in half over to the wrong side of the shade. At the base of the shade, fold the side borders in first and the base border over them. Fold and press under the outer edges of the base border diagonally, as shown, to finish neatly.*

5 *Secure the folded edges in place with slipstitch (see p. 44) and the side and base borders with herringbone stitch (see p. 44). Don't worry about the raw edges; they will be covered by the lining.*

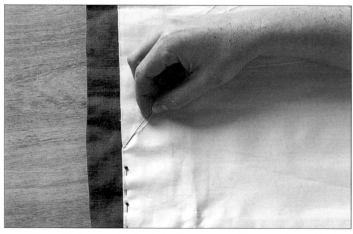

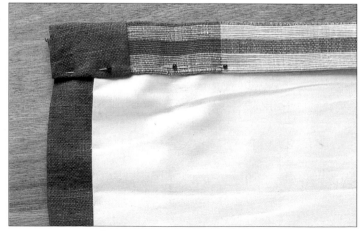

6 *Place lining on back of shade, wrong sides together. Tuck under raw edges and position as shown above, so that it covers the edges of the borders. Pin and slipstitch the lining in place along the sides and base of the shade.*

7 *Press over a ¾-in (2-cm) hem at the top of the shade, tucking under the raw edges of the fabric and lining as you go. Pin the hem in place at the top and secure with slipstitch.*

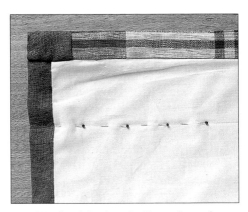

8 *Mark with pins the line where the slot will be folded over. This foldline will be the top of the finished shade.*

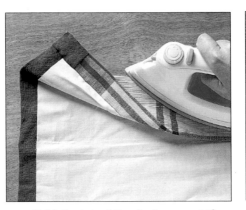

9 *Fold the top of the shade over at the marked line to make the slot. Press the slot section in place.*

10 *Pin the slot in place on the wrong side of the shade and slipstitch along the base to secure.*

Making the rod pocket and cording the shade

1 *Attach the rings to the back of the shade. Make two vertical rows, each set in 4 in (10 cm) from the sides of the shade. Set the lowest ring in each row 6 in (15 cm) above the top of the base border. Set the remaining rings about 6 in (15 cm) apart. Calculate the position of the rings upward from the lowest ring, with the highest ring being at least 8 in (20 cm) from the top.*

Slot heading
Screw eyes attached to top of window frame

Side border

Cords

Brass ring

Rod pocket with rod inside

Brass drop weight

Base border

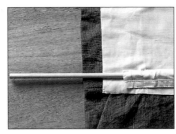

2 *Make the rod pocket (see Steps 1–3, p. 98) and pin and stitch it to the back of the shade just above the base of the lining. Insert the dowel rod into the pocket.*

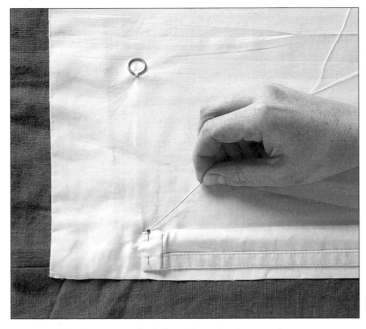

3 *Finish the open end of the rod pocket by turning over a double ⅜-in (1-cm) hem and securing with slipstitch. When stitched, both ends should align vertically with the rows of rings 4 in (10 cm) in from either side of the shade.*

4 *Thread a length of cord through each of the rows of rings at the back of the shade (see p. 54). Once the shade is up on its pole, thread the cords through screw eyes mounted in the window frame and into a drop weight.*

UNLINED SHADE WITH BORDERS

ALTHOUGH SIMILAR IN CONSTRUCTION to the Roman shade (see p. 96), this shade has a very different look. It has a cording mechanism that you use to raise and lower it, but the mechanism only operates down the sides and there are no rods across the back. When the shade is pulled up, its sides are left to swing in, creating an attractive scooped shape along the base.

The shade is also unlined, which lets the fabric fold more freely and allows light through during the day, and it has a crisp border that gives the edges added definition.

Type of window

• This shade works well on windows that are flat to the wall, provided there is sufficient space on either side, or on recessed windows where the shade is face fixed. It is equally well suited to portrait windows and square-shaped windows as well as to windows set side by side.
• This shade is useful for windows with unappealing views since, being unlined, it still allows light in when it is lowered. If you wish to block out all light while sleeping, fit a blackout roller shade behind it.

Type of fabric

• If you are making a small shade, avoid large patterns. Use stripes, checks, or small, pretty patterns. Alternatively, use strong plain colors for the main section and small patterns for the borders. Vary the border width, if necessary, to follow the width of a stripe or other pattern.
• Reversible fabrics, or fabrics with a definite front and back so the shade looks attractive from the outside, are also suitable.
• Avoid heavy fabrics, such as velvets and brocades, which would pull the sides of the shade in too much.

Options

• Two rows of rings set in from the sides of the shade give the scooped effect. If you add a central row of rings, the shade lifts in the center and alters the shape of the base.
• Deepen the border along the base and remove the side borders to create a different effect and emphasize the shape of the shade.
• Make a slot along the top of the shade and hang it from a pole.

WHAT YOU WILL NEED

Main fabric for shade

Width
Finished width of shade (see pp. 38–39), less twice the width of the border, plus 1½ in (4 cm) for seam allowances

Length
Finished drop of shade (see pp. 38–39), plus ¾ in (2 cm) for the base hem, plus 10 in (25 cm) for attaching the top to the lath

Border fabric for shade

Side (vertical) borders
2 borders, each the cut drop of the shade by twice the finished border width, plus 1½ in (4 cm) for seam allowances

Width of the border shown here is 2 in (5 cm)

Base (horizontal) border
The cut width of the shade, plus twice the cut width of a side border by the finished border width, plus 1½ in (4 cm) for seam allowances

Accessories

Lath
2 x 1-in (5 x 2.5-cm) timber lath cut to the finished width of shade

Brass rings
Finished drop of the shade, divided by 6 (if working in inches) or 15 (if working in centimeters), multiplied by 2

Screw eyes
3

Polyester cord
Enough for twice the drop of the shade, plus the width, multiplied by the number of rows of rings (see p. 54)

Brass drop weight and cleat

Making the shade

1 *Lay one border piece on top of the right-hand side of the fabric, with right sides together. Align and machine-stitch it to the fabric ¾ in (2 cm) in from the edge. Repeat with left-hand side and then attach the base border, running the stitching across the side borders.*

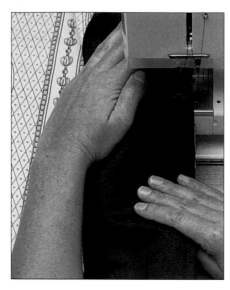

2 *Place the shade right side down and press the raw edges of the seams toward the borders.*

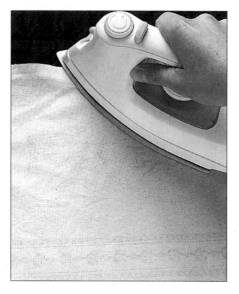

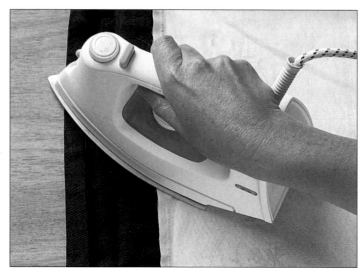

3 *With right sides still down, fold over the raw edges of both the side borders and the base border of the shade by ¾ in (2 cm) and press.*

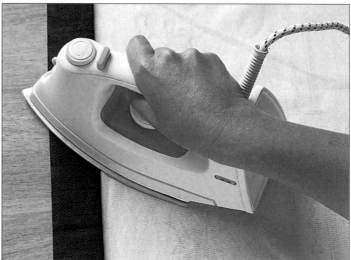

4 *Fold the side borders in, just covering the seam where the border is attached to the main fabric. Press and pin.*

Side border

Base border

5 *Fold the base border in to where the side borders meet it, making a neat edge. Press and pin.*

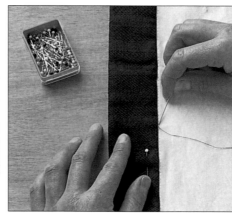

6 *Slipstitch (see p. 44) the side borders and the base border to the main fabric on the wrong side and remove the pins.*

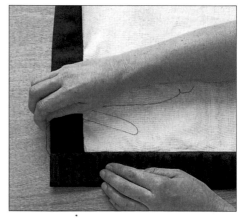

7 *Slipstitch the outer edges of the base border where it overlaps side borders. To fit the lath and screw eyes to the top of the shade, follow instructions on p. 55.*

Cording the shade

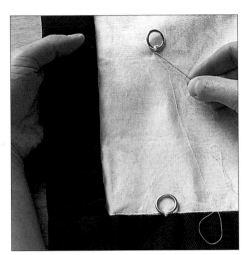

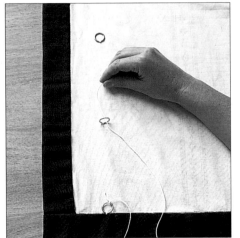

1 *Stitch the rings to the back of the shade. Make two vertical rows, each 4 in (10 cm) from the sides of the shade. Set the lowest ring just above the base border. Set the rest 6 in (15 cm) apart, working upward from the lowest ring.*

2 *Tie one length of cord to the lowest ring in the left-hand row. Thread through the rings and through the screw eye at the top. Take another cord and repeat with the second row (see p. 54).*

3 *After checking that both loose ends are the same length, thread both cords through the brass drop weight and secure them with a strong knot. Trim the ends of the cord and fix the shade in position (see pp. 56–57).*

VARIATION ON UNLINED SHADE WITH BORDERS

Set in front of a tall, elegant window recess, this unlined shade is made of a beautiful toile de Jouy print in unusual colors. As well as having no borders, it has a slightly different cording mechanism, with a central cord in addition to the two side cords. This levels the base, making it appear more like a standard Roman shade, but the absence of rods keeps the shade informal. As the shade folds up, it creates a shallow scoop on each side of the center, lending a hint of softness to the shape. The cording mechanism here incorporates a tape sewn through all layers. This creates a slight gathered effect that adds to the visual appeal.

INVERTED-PLEAT SHADE

A SMART, TAILORED SHADE, this is essentially a panel divided by a central inverted pleat. Both the colorful pleat and the matching flat border across the top add definition to the shade. A length of curtain tape is fitted to the back of the pleat and pulled up to give the base of the shade a scooped shape.

Type of window

• This style of shade needs to be long to look its best and works well on tall, narrow windows. It is suited to being held within an elegant frame or recess.

• The shade looks good pulled up only part way, forming soft folds and leaving much of the window permanently covered with fabric. Consider using this style of shade on a window that is not an important natural light source or on one that looks out onto an unattractive view that would be better concealed.

Type of fabric

• For the best effect, use two different but compatible fabrics, such as cottons of a similar weight. Because it creases so easily, linen is less suitable, unless you want a more casual "crumpled" look.

• Chenille or wool fabrics give a softer, weightier look to this shade. Alternatively, sheer fabrics, even flimsy muslins, look stunning and let light through.

• Choose patterns that still work well when divided by the pleat. On the divided sections, the patterns must match perfectly where they meet.

• Floral patterns inspired by classical Italian damasks suit this shade. Use smaller patterns or plain fabrics for the contrast pleat and border.

Options

• Instead of fixing the shade to a lath, make the border into a slot or sleeve for a pole. Allow space around the shade, both for pole fittings and for maximum impact, and add decorative finials.

• Deepen the border across the top to emphasize the length of the shade. Add a line of covered piping or chunky cord between the border and the main section of the shade to add texture and further contrast.

WHAT YOU WILL NEED

Main fabric for shade

Width
Finished width of shade (see pp. 38–39), plus 4 in (10 cm) for side hems, plus 1½ in (4 cm) for seams for joining to central pleat. Once cut, the fabric is cut in half again lengthwise

Length
Finished drop of the shade (see pp. 38–39), plus 2¾ in (7 cm) for hems, plus 10 in (25 cm) for fullness in the base of the shade

Fabric for pleat and border

Width for pleat
Twice the fullness of the pleat (see p. 41), plus 1½-in (4-cm) seam allowances for joining to main shade fabric

Length for pleat
As for main fabric

Width for border
Finished width of shade, plus 1½ in (4 cm) for seams

Length for border
Depth of border, plus ¾ in (2 cm) for hems, plus 10 in (25 cm) for rolling around lath

Lining fabric for shade and border

Width for shade lining
Finished width of shade, plus twice the fullness of the pleat

Length for shade lining
As for main fabric

Width for border lining
As for border

Length for border lining
As for border

Accessories

Tape
1-in (2.5-cm) tape cut to finished drop of shade

Rings
Finished drop of the shade, divided by 6 (if working in inches) or 15 (if working in centimeters), multiplied by 2

Lath
2 x 1-in (5 x 2.5-cm) timber lath cut to the finished width of shade

Screw eyes
3

Polyester cord
Enough for twice the drop of the shade, plus the width, multiplied by 2 (see p. 54)

Brass drop weight and cleat

Making the shade

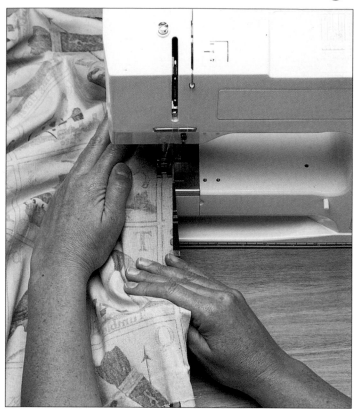

1 Pin and machine-stitch the contrasting pleat fabric to each section of the main fabric, right sides together, with ³⁄₄-in (2-cm) seams. You will then have one large piece, with the pleat fabric in the center and the two sections of main fabric on either side.

2 Press the seams toward the pleat so that they will not show from the front when the shade is hung. If your main fabric is darker than the pleat fabric, press the seams the other way.

Pressed line of side hem   Pressed line of base hem

Base hem pressed in

3 With the fabric still right side down, press over 2-in (5-cm) hems at the sides and base of the shade. Unfold the pressed hems and fold and press in each corner diagonally, aligning the pressed lines of the hems.

4 Turn the base hem in again and then the side hem (see inset) so that the folds meet. Slipstitch (see p. 44) them together and then secure the base and side hems with herringbone stitch (see p. 44).

5 Place the lining on the shade fabric wrong sides together. Press over the raw edges and pin in place so that the edge of the lining is ³⁄₈ in (1 cm) in from the sides of the main fabric.

6 *Slipstitch the lining in place on the back of the shade down both of the sides.*

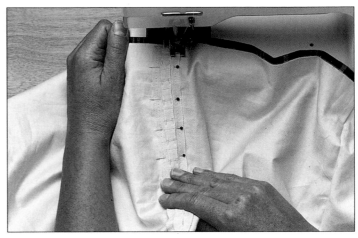

7 *Take a length of 1-in (2.5-cm) tape and pin it down the center of the pleat on the wrong side of the shade. Machine-stitch the tape to the shade through all layers.*

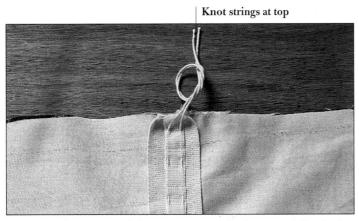

Knot strings at top

8 *Keep the strings of the tape open at the bottom of the shade, but knot them securely at the top.*

9 *With the shade right side up, mark a line down the center of the pleated section and fold the main fabric into this line to form the pleat. Pin and press the pleat into position.*

Attaching the border

1 *Place the border lining right side down and place the shade on top of it wrong side down, aligning the top of the shade with a long edge of the border lining. Then place the border fabric on top of the shade, right side down. The border lining and border will both extend 2 in (5 cm) on both sides of the shade.*

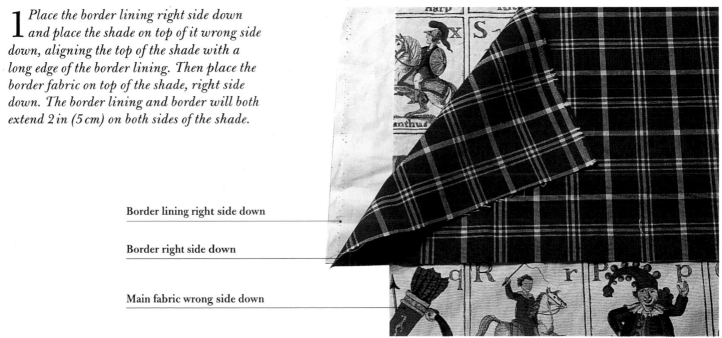

Border lining right side down

Border right side down

Main fabric wrong side down

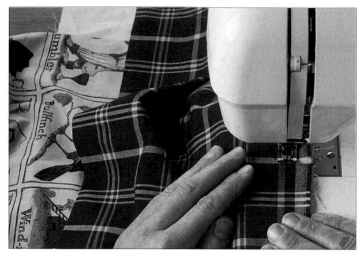

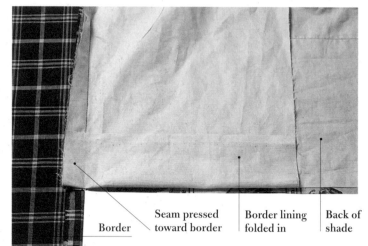

Border   Seam pressed   Border lining   Back of
toward border   folded in   shade

2 *Pin the three layers together across the top with a ¾-in (2-cm) seam and machine-stitch. Keep the folded pleat carefully in position. The stitching also secures the tape – make sure the knot is on the border side of the stitching line.*

3 *With the shade right side down, bring out the border from underneath it. Fold in the lining on both sides so that it aligns with the edge of the shade and press the seam toward the border.*

Border folded in

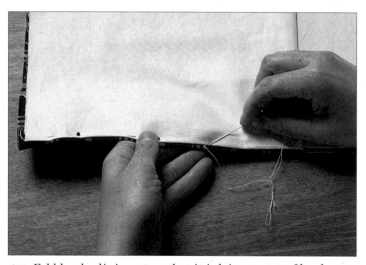

4 *Fold in border on each side in the same way as the lining so that it also aligns with edge of shade and press.*

5 *Fold border lining up so that it is lying on top of border, wrong sides together, and slipstitch the sides together.*

Cording the shade

1 *Attach rings to back of shade in two vertical rows, each 4 in (10 cm) from sides of shade. Set lowest one in each row 2 in (5 cm) from base of shade. Set each ring about 12 in (30 cm) above the other. Spacing will vary with drop of shade but should not be less than this. Calculate upward from lowest ring.*

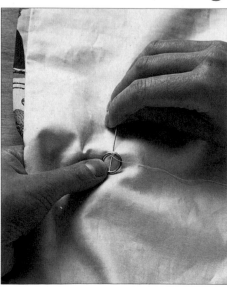

2 *Attach the lath and screw eyes to the top of the shade (see p. 54) and thread a length of cord through each row of rings, through the screw eyes, and into a brass drop weight (see p. 54).*

Pulling up the tape

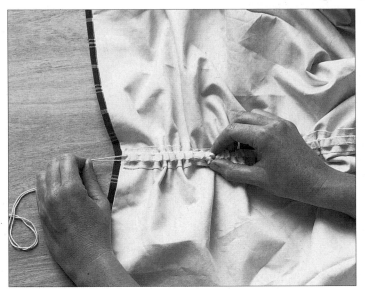

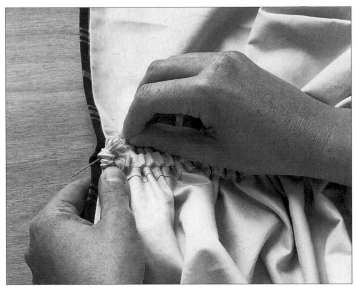

1 *Pull on the central tape to give some fullness at the base of the shade. The amount will depend on individual taste, but on average, pull up by 8–10 in (20–25 cm).*

2 *Knot the tape cords together to keep them from unraveling. Hand-sew the knot to the back of the shade so that it does not show from the front and hang the shade (see p. 57).*

VARIATION ON INVERTED-PLEAT SHADE

Instead of having just one central pleat, this shade has three, dividing it into four flat sections. The cording mechanism – one row of rings in the middle and one on each side – pulls the shade up into two "scoops." The pleats are similar to tucks and not very full. They catch the light, creating long thin shadows on the surface of the shade. Clever shaping at the top of the shade adds an elegance offset by the black painted molding.

LINED AND PLEATED SHADE

INVERTED PLEATS, evenly spaced across the width, emphasize the strong, clean lines of this shade and add fullness and form along the base. Cording is threaded through rows of rings set directly behind each pleat, so that soft folds form between the pleats as the shade is pulled up. This style of shade should be fitted to a lath, not hung from a pole, but it may be placed inside or outside a window recess.

Type of window

• This shade is best for windows with a horizontal shape, such as the example shown here. It adds softness to this type of featureless, deep-recessed casement.
• Avoid long portrait windows for this shade. The inverted pleats make a lot of fabric and a long shade would be difficult to raise and lower.
• If a window has vertical bars, use them as a guide for positioning the pleats, but do not follow them too rigidly. The shade looks better with some asymmetry.

Type of fabric

• You can use almost any fabric for this shade, but those that emphasize the shape, such as strong plain colors, stripes, or checks, are better than fabrics with busy overall patterns. The classic striped fabric used here provides just enough pattern and color, without interfering with the sculptured shape of the shade.
• Crisp cotton and lightweight canvas both pleat well and are not too bulky when pulled up.
• Beware of fabrics with a pattern across the width for this shade. Ensure that any pattern chosen still works when the pleats are formed.
• For added interest, try using a contrast lining in a color darker than the main fabric. Some diffused color will show through when light shines through the shade.

Options

• Sew a fringe across the base of the shade to add texture and interest (see p. 29), but keep the fringe in style with the fabric and surroundings. On the shade shown here, for example, a chunky jute fringe would be more suitable than an ornate silky style with delicate tassels.
• To add depth and contrast, try making the pleats in a fabric different from the main shade.

WHAT YOU WILL NEED

Main fabric for shade

Width

Finished width of shade (see pp. 38–39), plus 4 in (10 cm) for the side hems, plus amount for each pleat (see p. 41 for calculating pleats), plus 4 in (10 cm) for returns

Length

Finished drop of shade (see pp. 38–39), plus 2 in (5 cm) for the base hem, plus 10 in (25 cm) for fullness at the base of the shade, plus 2 in (5 cm) for attaching the top to the lath

Lining fabric for shade

Width

As for main fabric, minus 4 in (10 cm)

Length

As for main fabric, minus 2 in (5 cm)

For covering lath

Enough fabric to cover the lath completely including the ends (see p. 55)

Accessories

Brass rings

Finished drop of shade, divided by 6 (if working in inches) or 15 (if working in centimeters), multiplied by number of pleats plus 2

Lath

2 x 1-in (5 x 2.5-cm) timber lath cut to finished width of shade and covered with lining fabric (see p. 56)

Screw eyes

As number of pleats, plus 3

Polyester cord

Twice drop of shade plus width, multiplied by the number of pleats plus 2 (see p. 54)

Brass drop weight and cleat

Making the shade

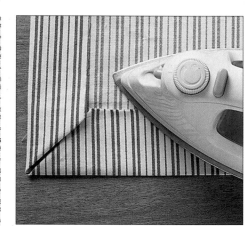

Side hem folded out

Aligned hems

Base corner folded in

Aligned hems

Base hem folded out

1 *With right side down, press over a single 2-in (5-cm) hem down both sides of the main fabric and along the base. Fold the side and base hems back out and fold in each base corner diagonally, aligning the pressed lines of the hems as shown.*

2 *Press the base and side hems back into place, making mitered corners. Make sure that the pattern matches up neatly where the side and base hems meet. Pin the corners in place.*

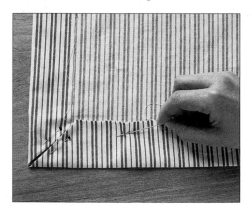

3 *Secure the side and base hems of the shade with herringbone stitch (see p. 44) and the mitered corners with slipstitch (see p. 44).*

Attaching the lining

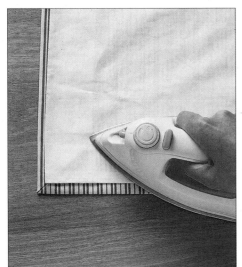

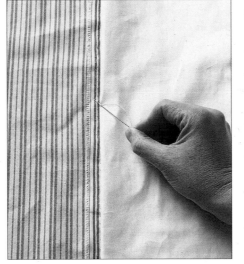

1 *Place the lining fabric onto the back of the shade, wrong sides together. Fold under the raw edges of the lining along the bottom and sides so that it is about ⅜ in (1 cm) in from the edges of the shade. Press and pin it in place.*

2 *If you are making a shade as wide as the one here – finished width of 72 in (183 cm) – lock in the lining (see p. 44) across the shade at width and half-width intervals (see p. 43).*

3 *Slipstitch (see p. 44) the lining in place along the sides and the base of the shade. Leave the top open.*

Making the pleats

1 *To mark the position of the pleats, measure from one edge the width between each pleat plus 2 in (5 cm) for the return, and mark with a vertical line of pins. Here, the width between each pleat is 18 in (45 cm).*

2 *Measure from there the amount allowed for a pleat (see p. 41) and mark with a vertical line of pins. Here, 6 in (15 cm) is allowed for each pleat.*

3 *Next, measure and mark the next space between pleats – without 2 in (5 cm) for the return – and then the next pleat. Continue across the shade until you reach the other side, where you finish as you started, with a space between pleats plus 2 in (5 cm) for the return.*

4 *To provide guides for folding the pleats, measure and mark with another pin the center spot between the first and second lines of pins.*

5 *Measure and mark the space between the third and fourth lines of pins in the same way, and continue across the shade until you have measured and marked all of the pleats.*

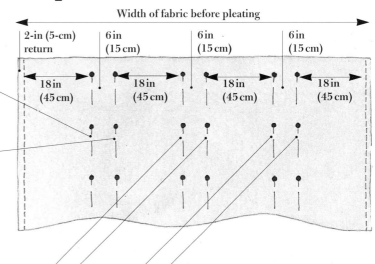

Width of fabric before pleating

2-in (5-cm) return   6 in (15 cm)   6 in (15 cm)   6 in (15 cm)

18 in (45 cm)   18 in (45 cm)   18 in (45 cm)   18 in (45 cm)

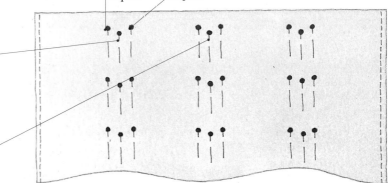

First line of pins   Second line of pins

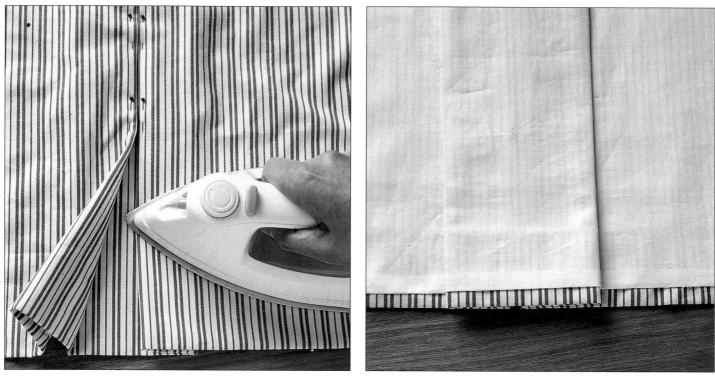

6 *Starting with the first three lines of pins, fold the fabric so that the first line of pins meets the second line. Then fold in the other side so that the third line of pins also meets the second line. Press the folds in place and repeat for other pleats.*

7 *When you have pressed all the pleats, turn over the shade and check that all the pleats are straight and neatly pressed in place. Repeat the process if necessary.*

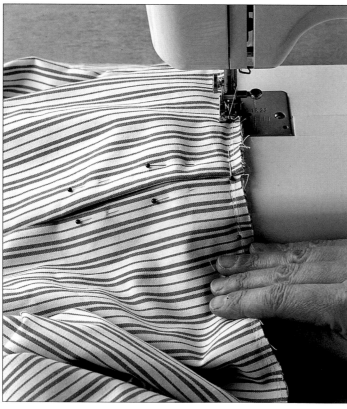

8 *Turn the shade right side up and machine-stitch along the top of the shade to secure the pleats in position. Make sure that you catch the lining.*

9 *Measure 2 in (5 cm) from the top of the shade and draw a pencil line across the shade on the lining side. Machine-stitch across the top just above the line. This prevents the pleats from unfolding when the top of the shade is rolled around the lath.*

Cording the shade

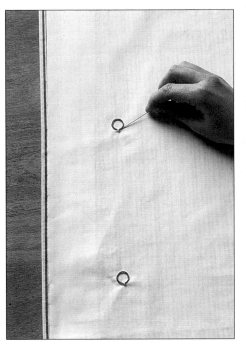

1 *Position and stitch in place by hand the rows of rings up the back of the shade (see p. 54). Position the bottom ring 2 in (5 cm) from the bottom edge of the shade and then at approximately 6-in (15-cm) intervals. Have one row 4 in (10 cm) in from each side of the shade and one row running up the center of each pleat.*

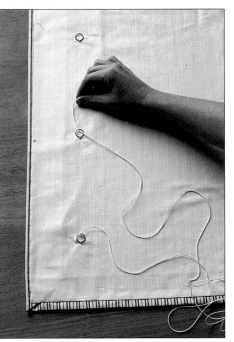

2 *Attach the lath to the top of the shade (see p. 56) and fit screw eyes (see p. 55), aligning them with the rows of rings below. Thread the cords through the rings, screw eyes, and brass drop weight and secure them with a strong knot (see p. 54). You can now hang the shade (see p. 57).*

VARIATION FOR LINED AND PLEATED SHADE

The fringe on this shade adds decoration and texture, and it accentuates the series of scoops along the base. The color of the fringe harmonizes with the fabric used for the shade and is in keeping with the simplicity of the shade's style.

FABRIC CARE

To MAKE YOUR curtains and shades last longer and look better, you should handle them as little as possible. Most fabrics will fade eventually, but you can delay the process by always drawing them back or up during the day unless, such as with sheer fabrics, they are specifically designed to remain drawn or down.

Cleaning

Always follow the manufacturer's recommendations when cleaning fabrics. Dry cleaning is the best option for shades and all but the simplest of curtains and, if possible, you should get them cleaned professionally rather than using commercial sprays. Some companies will come and clean curtains and shades on site and rehang them for you.

You can wash simple, unlined curtains, but remember that many fabrics will shrink, especially those made from natural fibers. Check whether the fabric is preshrunk (if in doubt you can wash and iron the fabric before making the curtains) and make sure you leave an adequate hem that can be let down if necessary.

Never wash interlined curtains and only wash lined curtains when the lining is detachable. The lining fabric and main fabric may shrink by different amounts and the curtains may lose body and finish.

Only wash shades if the fabric is preshrunk and you are certain it will not shrink any more. Remove any brass rings, cording, and dowel rods first.

Dealing with Stains

You may be able to deal with any small stains on the spot. Blot away as much of the stain as possible and use a commercial stain remover. Test it first on an unobtrusive corner of fabric. Avoid using water on silk or wool as it can cause discoloration and shrinkage.

GLOSSARY

Architrave brackets: slim brackets, usually made of brass, fitted to the wall or window frame and used to support a pole.

Batting: a fluffy, fibrous material used to stuff goblet pleats (see p. 51).

Blackout lining: a special lining that blocks out all light. It is made of a layer of opaque material between two layers of cotton fabric (see p. 32).

Box pleats: a hand-sewn heading of flat pleats made at the front of a curtain (see p. 51).

Bradawl: a pointed tool used for making holes for screw eyes in a wooden lath.

Brocade: a heavy fabric, woven to create raised patterns and including some gold or silver thread. It was traditionally made in silk, but modern brocades are also available in cotton.

Buckram: stiffened fabric used to give shape to pleated headings. Fusible buckram can be sealed to the fabric by the heat of an iron.

Café clip: decorative clip that grips the top of a curtain or shade and encircles a pole support.

Calico: a raw unbleached cotton fabric with a plain weave (see p. 32).

Chenille: a soft fabric made from fluffy cotton yarn (see p. 33).

Chintz: a fabric usually made from cotton and generally printed with floral patterns on a cream or light ground (see p. 35).

Cleat: metal hook fixed to one side of a window and used to secure the cords of a shade when it is pulled up.

Cording: a system of cords threaded through rings fitted to the back of a shade so that it can be raised and lowered (see p. 54).

Cut drop: the finished drop of a curtain or shade plus allowances for hems and headings.

Cut width: the finished width of a curtain or shade plus allowances for seams and fullness for the heading.

Damask: a woven fabric with a special weave that produces a raised pattern and flat background (see pp. 33–35). Damask is made in different fibers, such as wool, silk, and cotton.

Dowel rod: a slender wooden rod that is inserted into fabric pockets at the back of a shade, such as the Roman shade (see p. 96), enabling it to be pulled up in neat folds.

Drop weight: a holder made of brass or wood into which the cords of a shade are threaded.

Eyelets: a two-part metal ring used as a heading for curtains or shades. A punch and dye set punches a hole in the fabric and fits the two parts of the eyelet, one on each side of the fabric.

Finial: decorative end pieces fitted to a pole (see p. 16) to provide a visual finishing touch and to keep the rings on the pole.

Finished drop: the length of a curtain or shade once it is made and hung.

Finished dropline: the point that marks the finished length of a curtain or shade.

Finished width: the width of the area a curtain or shade is to cover. The curtain or shade should make this width once it is pleated or gathered.

French pleats: also known as pencil pleats, this heading is made up of groups of three slim pleats spaced across the curtain. The pleats can be made with special heading tape but look better if hand-sewn (see p. 50).

Gingham: a simple, checked fabric made of cotton.

Goblet pleats: a hand-sewn heading made of rounded pleats that are stuffed with batting so they keep their shape (see p. 51).

Heading: the finish at the top of a curtain or shade. Headings range from simple gathered headings made with tape to more complex pleated headings (see pp. 18–19).

Herringbone: fabric with a diagonally patterned weave (see p. 33).

Hessian: an open-weave, rough-textured fabric made of fiber from the jute plant (see p. 33).

Interlining: a combed cotton fabric placed between the main fabric of a curtain or shade and the lining to provide insulation and body.

Lath: a piece of timber, usually 2 x 1 in (5 x 2.5 cm), to which the top of a shade is fitted. The lath is then attached to the wall, ceiling, or window frame (see p. 15).

Lath and fascia: a structure fitted in front of a curtain track to conceal it. The lath is fitted at right angles to the wall and the fascia fitted to the front of it. Track is fitted to the underside of the lath and is concealed by the fascia (see p. 15). The lath and fascia are generally covered in the same fabric as the curtains.

Lining: a cotton fabric used to back curtains and shades (see p. 32).

Mitering: a technique used to make a neat, flat corner where the side hem and base hem of a curtain or shade meet (see p. 46).

Muslin: a fine, translucent cotton. Most muslin is plain but some have a white printed design to add texture (see p. 33).

Pelmet: a panel, made of wood or fabric stiffener and covered with fabric, that hides the top of a curtain. The pelmet is fixed to a wooden support fixed above the curtain track.

Pencil pleats: *see* French pleats.

Piping: a neat, practical finish for the edges of curtains and shades made from strips of fabric cut on the bias (diagonally across the fabric) and stitched around lengths of cord.

Poplin: a light, cotton fabric with a corded surface made by using thicker weft threads than warp threads.

Punch and dye set: *see* Eyelets.

Recess window: a window that is set back into the wall, so that you can hang a curtain or shade inside the recess instead of on the wall.

Return: the part of a curtain or shade that goes around the end of a track or lath.

Self-pelmet: fabric at the top of a curtain that is folded and stitched to look like a separate section.

Selvage: the tightly woven edges of a width of fabric.

Slot heading: a simple sleeve of fabric stitched at the top of a curtain or shade into which you slide a slim pole as a support (see p. 48).

Support: a device, such as a pole, track, or lath, from which a curtain or shade hangs. It can be attached outside, on, or within the frame.

Tapestry: a heavy, machine-woven fabric that imitates the look of traditional hand-woven tapestries (see p. 34).

Thermal lining: cotton lining fabric that is coated with a layer of aluminum on one side for insulation.

Tieback: a device made of fabric, rope, ribbon, or other material used to tie a curtain back.

Toile de Jouy: a cotton fabric originally made in the French town of Jouy and printed with scenes of country life.

Voile: a white, semitransparent fabric made of silk or cotton.

Warp threads: the threads of a fabric that travel up and down.

Weft threads: the threads of a fabric that travel from side to side.

Weights: round metal discs that are placed in the hems of curtains to help them hang better.

Width of fabric: the width of the fabric as purchased. Most furnishing fabric comes in widths of 54 in (140 cm) or 48 in (120 cm). Generally, the width of fabric you use is less than the cut width of your curtain or shade and so you need to buy more than one width and join them together.

INDEX

ACKNOWLEDGMENTS

There are many who supplied or lent their products or services during the making of this book. The publisher and author would like to thank the following for their invaluable support.

Jacqui Badham and Caroline Badham
Paine & Co.
Kate and Paul Turner

Fabrics and trimmings
Abbott & Boyd
Bennison Fabrics
Designers Guild
Hodsoll McKenzie
Ian Mankin
Ian Sanderson
Isle Mill
Nobilis Fontan
Osborne & Little
Percheron
Pierre Frey (UK) Ltd.
Ramm Son & Crocker
Watts & Co.
Zoffany

Poles and accessories
Byron & Byron
McKinney & Co.

Furniture and furnishings
Castle Gibson
Crucial Trading
D. A. Binder
David Champion
Josephine Ryan

Flooring
Crucial Trading
Fired Earth
Lassco
Sinclair Till

Lights
Sitch & Co.

The publisher and author would also like to thank the following sources for their kind permission to reproduce the photographs listed right.

Ianthe Ruthven: 14 left, 23 top, 63 bottom.

Elizabeth Whiting and Associates
June Buck: 27 top right.
Michael Dunne: 117 bottom.
Brian Harrison: 89 bottom right (des: David Rone Allan).
Andreas von Einsiedel: 15 left (des: Jo Robinson). 123 bottom.

International Interiors
Paul Ryan: 20 top (des: Jan des Bouvrie), 26 top (des: Pet Boon).

Marie Claire Maison
Gille de Chabaneix: 22 top (styl: Daniel Rozensztroch).
Nicholas Tosi: 95 bottom right (styl: Julie Borgeaud).

Robert Harding Picture Library
IPC Magazines/Jan Baldwin: 111 bottom.
Chris Drake: 19 top.
Gavin Kingcome: 17 top right.
Polly Wreford: 13 top right, 15 top.

The Interior Archive
Tim Beddow: 18 top (des: Dido Farrell).
Tim Clinch: 30 top (des: Nacho James).
Fritz von der Schulenberg: 14 (des: Emily Todhunter), 21 top (des: Christophe Gollut), 24 top (des: Alidad), 25 top, 28 top (des: Christophe Gollut), 67 bottom left and right, 73 bottom (des: Kath Kidston), 95 bottom left (des: Mimmi O'Connell).